INDUSTRIES
FOR SMALL COMMUNITIES

With Cases from Yellow Springs

THE YELLOW SPRING   *Photo by Axel*

    This large, iron bearing spring gave the village its name. Measurements through more than a century record an unvarying flow. By deposit of iron and lime it has built itself to a height of 50 feet or more above the valley bottom. Estimates indicate that it has been building this deposit for about 40,000 years since the last glacial period.

INDUSTRIES FOR
SMALL COMMUNITIES

With Cases from Yellow Springs

BY

ARTHUR E. MORGAN

Former President, Antioch College
Former Chairman, Tennessee Valley Authority
President, Community Service, Inc.

☙

COMMUNITY SERVICE, INCORPORATED
Yellow Springs, Ohio

Printed in the U.S.A.

EDWARDS BROTHERS, INC.
Ann Arbor, Michigan

CONTENTS

Chapter I

WHY TELL THE STORY

The book *Middletown*, by Robert and Helen Lynd, published in 1929, acquainted the general American public with the idea of using a somewhat detailed study of a single city to throw light on social conditions. More than half a century earlier the great French sociologist, Le Play, established this method of inquiry by his now famous studies of the lives and budgets of individual workingmen in various parts of Europe. We learn best by cases. This story of the little industries of a midwestern town is of interest, not chiefly as the annals of a small progressive community, but as throwing light on certain new trends and possibilities in American economic life of which the public seems to be but dimly aware.

Many a small town in America sees added industrial income as a critical need. But what can they do about it? How can a community actually increase its industrial activity and income? Visit a hundred small towns and we will find a general similarity in the local outlooks as to the problem of securing industries. The most usual course is for the local civic club or chamber of commerce or a committee of business men to search for one which can be persuaded to locate in the community. Frequently such incentives are provided as free location, remittance of local taxes for five or ten years, or the purchase of a block of stock. Hundreds, perhaps thousands, of American small towns have records of securing industries by such enticements, only to have them fail and leave. Yet such search for industries does not always fail. Responsible companies looking for locations may ask for some such evidence of interest as a way of making sure that they are wanted.

These conventional methods have been almost totally absent in Yellow Springs. A farmer's village of less than 1500 people, with a very small liberal college, and with almost no industrial life, in the course of two or three decades has become the location of a dozen extremely varied industries, with more than 500 regular employees on its payrolls, and with annual sales of its products of about $7,000,000. In addition, about a dozen economic undertakings including industrial design, an advertising agency, wholesale distributors, contractors and others have developed businesses there.

As big business goes in America that is very "small pickings,"
yet to this small community it means a large increase in the
number and variety of ways for its young people to make a
living; it means added tax income, a greater variety of
personal and cultural interests, and the greater degree of
security which tends to be the result of variety of sources
of income. It is of interest that all of these little industries are independent, and are locally owned.

A story of just what happened and how it happened may be
suggestive to individuals and to communities who are wonder-
ing how to get a toehold in business or industry. Not that
identical methods should be used elsewhere, but that certain
general points of view and policies may be applicable. The
stories of these little industries are given in some detail
so that the reader may get a feel of how they came into
being. Perhaps only one or two may describe circumstances
similar to his own, though some others will almost certainly
provide suggestions. General discussion of principles and
policies will not give the same intimate feel of how things
can be done as will a direct account of how actual undertakings have been carried on.

Quite frequently people who would promote small industry
have thought of it as a going back to earlier and simpler
ways of living. They fight against the inexorable trend of
economic life toward greater complexity. They do not want to
admit that we are moving from an economy based on small power
generating units to power plants on a constantly larger scale;
from natural materials to a world of synthetics; from an age
of easy tolerance in our mechanical and chemical production
to rigorous enforcement of exacting standards of manufacture;
from relative independence of action in economic life to
increasing interdependence. The typical friend of little
industry hesitates to admit that industry based on old-time
simplicity continues to shrink and fade, and that the small
industry of the future will exist and thrive, not in spite
of these modern trends, but because of them. For three decades or more we have heard the constantly repeated assertion
that whereas there was a time when a man of small means could
start a new industry, that day is past, and that now only the
possession of considerable means would justify a person in
attempting such a venture. Yet it has been during this period
that all these little industries of Yellow Springs have been

started, and the rate of beginning has increased through the years. For these reasons we believe that their stories are worth telling in some detail.

Those who see big business as coming to have a monopoly of our economic life are similarly living in the economic climate of decades past. Because big business is in the spotlight, and because great new consolidations continue to appear, the impression is abroad that it makes up American business. This opinion is characteristic of America as a whole and tends to discourage persons who otherwise might be inclined to create small industries or to be associated with them. One of the greatest hinderances to the increase of American small business in many fields is not so much any inherent technical superiority of bigness as it is the mental climate of industrial America. Bigness, whether in industries, in government or in universities, is uncritically worshipped.

Taken all together, small industry has a very large field of action, in making goods for sale directly to the consumer, in making parts or materials which enter into products made by big and little industry, and in making tools, instruments and other devices which other industries large and small need for making their products.

Interest in small industry does not imply that it ever could or should occupy the entire industrial field. More than 15 years ago I said that:

America, I hoped, would become like one of our great forests that I visited recently. There were trees one and two centuries old towering a hundred feet overhead; underneath them was another level of trees—ironwoods, sourwood, birches—growing half as high, filling in the interstices where the sunlight was not being used by the larger trees. Then another order of trees—hawthorns, dogwood, and sassafras—filled in the unoccupied places in the more humble positions. Next below were shrubs—viburnums and laurel - and beneath them blueberry bushes and smaller plants only a few feet high; and still underneath came a whole population of flowers that get their sunshine and do their year's work early in the spring before the leaves are out on the trees, and while the sun can shine through. These included such flowers as the trillium, hepatica, and anemones. Then down on the ground and on the tree trunks were mosses and lichens. That whole variety was included in the forest.

> *We sometimes think of the trees overhead as enduring,*
> *and of the smaller plants below as transient; yet it is*
> *probably true that some ground plants, such as trilliums,*
> *are older than the trees above. Some of these plants*
> *develop a new bit of rootstock each year while the*
> *oldest part decays. Barring accidents, such a plant may*
> *live for centuries.*
>
> *My picture of American business is not of a choice*
> *between big business and little business, but of normal*
> *distribution, just as there is normal distribution*
> *between large and small in a primeval hardwood forest.*
> *Let that which is most effective if big remain big, that*
> *which is most effective if middle-sized remain middle-*
> *sized, and that which is most effective if small remain*
> *small; each respecting the functions of the other.*

The general aim of public policy in reference to industry should be that neither bigness nor smallness shall be arbitrarily promoted or maintained by special privilege, coercion, repression, or inertia. Two generations ago there were many small industries which could not reach their best efficiency without growing larger. Today there may be many industrial products made by large industrial corporations which, all things considered, could be better produced by small, independent industry.

An account of Yellow Springs little industries suggests general areas in American industry in which promising prospects are likely to be found. For the most part the men who began these undertakings were interested in what America would be doing tomorrow, not what it was doing yesterday.

Along with descriptions of little industries we have included accounts of certain other activities, not because an industrial art studio or an advertising agency is properly to be classed as an industry, but because such accounts help to fill out the picture of personal initiative and economic activity which provide sources of livelihood and contribute to the character and flavor of the community. They illustrate the variety of interests which makes Yellow Springs an interesting place to live, and which may be among the reasons why persons of ranging interests decide on the village for the location of their own projects.

Chapter II

IS SMALL INDUSTRY WORTH WHILE?

During the late 1920's I was visiting the president of one of the largest banks in New York when I introduced the subject of small industries. My host expressed himself forcefully on the subject and concluded by saying that the choice in America "is between big business and peanut stands." He implied that any person concerned with business who did not choose big business would be lacking ordinary common sense. Many Americans are of a similar opinion.

Yet small business does not die. Let me quote from a talk by Benjamin Fairless, President of the United States Steel Corporation. In addressing the Wharton School of Commerce of the University of Pennsylvania on November 12, 1951, he said:

> I refer you to an official release put out by the Defense Production Administration in Washington, and numbered D.P.A.-95. It shows that in the first nine months following the outbreak of the Korean War, small business increased its employment by twenty-three per cent, while big business enlarged its own working force by only fifteen per cent.

> We hear it said repeatedly that big business gets all the fat profits out of these defense contracts, while small business is forced to survive on the crumbs that fall from the table. Well, that isn't true either, so let me refer you to a government document called "The Quarterly Industrial Financial Report Series," put out by the F.T.C. and the S.E.C.

> This study covers all the manufacturing corporations in the United States, and divides them into five groups according to size--giving a complete financial report for each group. And here is what it shows:

> Between the first quarter of last year and the first quarter of this year the dollar profits of the smallest companies increased eleven times as fast as those of the biggest corporations. Among the smallest businesses, moreover, the rate of profit on sales rose 200 per cent; but among the biggest businesses it dropped more than thirteen per cent. And all along the line we find that-- no matter how we measure the profits--one thing always remains true: the smaller the firm, the larger the gain, in profits; the larger the firm, the smaller the gain, if any.

*Not even the biggest of these companies could fill a
single one of these government orders all by itself.
Each must buy raw assemblies from thousands of other
firms of every size and description.*

*To turn out its planes, for example, the aircraft in-
dustry will have to use sixty thousand sub-contractors
and suppliers; and sixty per cent of these sub-contracts
will go to small business. General Electric will use
17,000 sub-contractors and suppliers and will pay them
more than half the money it gets from the government for
its defense work. General Motors found, during the last
war, that it had to call on 19,000 other companies to
help it do the defense job. . . .*

*When just one of these hundred thousand orders comes
to the U.S. Steel Corp., for example, we, in turn, must
employ nearly 54,000 other companies to provide us with
the things we need in making the steel and cement that
is wanted. In fact, forty per cent of all the money we
take in each year is paid to these suppliers, and each
of them in his turn will pass part of the work and money
along to his suppliers.*

Similar statements of the reliance of big industries upon
little industries have been made recently by Dupont and by
General Motors. The little industries of Yellow Springs
illustrate this state of affairs. Some of the smallest of
them, with only a dozen or so employees, supply products
which the largest firms need, and cannot get elsewhere.

There are many other small industries in America the products of which do not enter directly into the complex current
which includes our large corporations. Many of these have
relatively independent cycles of their own. There is the
planing mill which finishes local lumber for local use, the
feed mill which grinds local grain for local farmers, the
local newspaper, and makers of endless products for individual
consumers, and which do not go into the making of some big-
industry product such as steel or airplanes or automobiles.

There is much evidence that small industry, when reasonably well managed, gets a fair part of the industrial profits.
In 1937 the Twentieth Century Fund, a competent and independent nonprofit research organization, published a study,
How Profitable Is Big Business. The data on which this study
was based were the *Statistics of Income* of the U.S. Bureau

of Internal Revenue, "by far the best source of data on the relationship between size and profits."

The conclusions of this study were that, while there are many variations in specific industries, by and large, small industries have larger profits than big ones. Manufacturing corporations were listed by the Bureau of Internal Revenue in 9 classes; the first, of those with less than $50,000 capital, the next, of those with $50,000 to $100,000, and on up to the last two, with capital of $10,000,000 to $50,000,000, and of more than $50,000,000.

Measuring net income as percentage of invested capital, in the year 1919 the profits for business with less than $50,000 capital were 27.8%. As business grew larger and capitalization increased, net income as a percentage of capital decreased steadily, to 9.7% for industries with capital of over $50,000,000.

For the depression years, 1931 to 1933, for businesses making a profit, in general the larger the capitalization the smaller the profit. On the other hand, for businesses losing money, the smaller the business the greater the loss. Kaplan* states that when business is on the upgrade small business profits increase faster than those of large businesses. When business is shrinking small business profits decrease faster. He reports that for small business it is customary to pay a considerable part of the earnings as salaries to officials, and to depreciate the plant much more heavily. As reported to the U.S. Bureau of Internal Revenue in 1941, for corporations with less than $50,000 capital, "compensation to officers totaled roughly 15 times the net profit. . . . All three of the classes up to $250,000 reported a larger amount for aggregate salaries to officers than the reported net profit." The general habit of paying profits as salaries, while showing operating deficits, confuses the statistical picture as to small business, and makes it seem less profitable than it is in fact.

The Twentieth Century Fund found that corporations of $50,000 to $100,000 capital depreciate their assets more than twice as fast as the group with the largest capitalization. If salaries of officers and depreciation are included

---

*"Small Business: Its Place and Problems," (McGraw-Hill, 1948).

in profits, the advantage of small industries is far more marked. Even of corporations showing no corporate earnings, when adjustments are made for officers' salaries and for depreciation and depletion, the smallest and next smallest classes of corporations have the highest rates of earnings, with the very largest class next.

The book, *How Profitable Is Big Business*, makes many statistical comparisons, showing great variations in different industries and under different conditions. Small businesses turn over their capital much more rapidly. In 1933 the annual rate of turnover of capital for the smallest and next smallest classes of business was 381% of the net worth for the smallest and 269% for the next smallest. For the next to the largest the annual turnover was 68%, and for the largest was only 57% of the net worth. Since rapid turnover of capital is generally favorable to profits, this is a marked advantage to small business.

Big industry seldom gets the full, reasonable productive effort of its workers. About 25 years ago, before the C.I.O. was organized, and before industry and business were very generally unionized, Antioch College in association with the Social Science Research Council made a study of limitation of production by nonunion workers, mostly in big business. A report of the study was published.* Non-union industry was chosen so as not to confuse the study with the union issue.

It was found that deliberate, substantial limitation of production was almost universal in the large industries studied. Sometimes a manager would advise that a study of his plant would be of no value as he had no restriction of output to contend with. Yet on making a study in that plant it would be found that restriction of production was purposely practiced and was consciously and often skillfully organized. A rough guess for industry in general was that the disappearance of deliberate restriction of output might increase production by more than 25%.

Recently a representative of a great American industry, on visiting one of our Yellow Springs firms and walking through its plant, remarked, "I see your shop is on piecework." When told that there was not a piecework job in the factory, but that all men were on regular hourly wages, he

---

*Mathewson, Stanley B., "Restriction of Output among Unorganized Workers" (New York, Viking Press, 1931).

remarked, "But men on hourly wages do not work as these men work." The better administered small industries may come closer to receiving the full, reasonable productive efforts of employees than does big industry. This factor alone might have much to do with the better profit position of well run small industry.

According to the Twentieth Century Fund report, big industry had the advantage that a much larger part of its capital is in common stock, on which no payments need be made when business is unfavorable. Small firms are much more frequently financed by short-term loans, and therefore are more likely to be closed out if profits temporarily fail. As a result, large businesses are commonly stabler and safer investments for the outsider, especially if he is not intimately acquainted with them.

The Twentieth Century Fund also reported on a number of other studies of the relative profits of large and small business, from which the following are summarized:

H.B. Summers compared rates of earnings of 1130 large and small industries in the United States and Canada.* He found the highest average earnings to be in the smallest of 9 classes (divided as previously described). Studying several major fields one by one, in no case was the largest earning in the class of largest industries. In 4 of 9 industrial groups size was more favorable to earnings than in the others. The author found that "with certain exceptions heavy investment is apparently a disadvantage in securing high rates of earnings."

In a study, *Corporate Earning Power*, in 1929, Crum and Bowman found "Rates of net income to total assets increase up to net income of $100,000, but not significantly thereafter."

Ralph P. Epstein in his *Industrial Profits in the United States* found for the years 1919 to 1938 that "Beyond question among manufacturing corporations of all sizes of capital from $250,000 to over $50,000,000, the smaller corporations earn profits at higher rates than the larger ones. . . . The class with capital of less than $500,000 showed a rate of return of more than 20%; the class with capital of $50,000,000 and over, of less than 10%."

---

*Quarterly Journal of Economics, May, 1932.

W.A. Paton, in *Corporate Profits as Shown by Audit Reports*, studies of 1927-29, showed that corporations with assets between $50,000 and $200,000 earned on the average at a higher rate on their assets than either smaller or larger ones.

The National Industrial Conference Board study, *Shifting and Effects of Federal Corporation Income Tax—1918-1925*, states that the most profitable group in each year had a smaller average capital than the average of all corporations studied.

Kaplan, in *Small Business: Its Place and Problems*, going over much the same source material in 1948, emphasized the confusing and sometimes conflicting data met with in making comparisons of profits of large and small business, and was more reserved in his conclusions than most of the authors we have quoted. However, the general inference was similar. From all the studies referred to it is clear that small industry is not the hopeless prospect that it is commonly considered, but when well managed earns at a higher rate than big industry.

To sum up the conclusions of the various studies which have been made, we find that there are many thousands of active small industries in our country. They are not chiefly surviving vestiges of a passing social order, but to a large degree are normal, integral elements of modern industrial life. They vary much more widely in their degree of success or failure than do large industries. They are the trying-out ground for industrial activity. Many were inadvisedly undertaken or never had good management and were unsuccessful from the start, and there is large elimination of those that are unfit, ill-timed, inappropriate, or unfortunate. Most large industries grew up from small ones, or are the results of combinations which had such small beginnings. Most elimination of the unfit occurred before they had become large.

Every increase in the area of technology enlarges the frontier along which new technical products or methods may emerge. For instance, the field of electronics, still in its infancy, has resulted in perhaps a thousand or more little industries to supply its ever-increasing needs for instruments, parts and materials. Laboratory equipment is another promising field for small scale operations. A single dealer lists more than 20,000 items, many of them products of small industries. Many of these are not articles made entirely by a single manufacturer. Some of them are assemblies of parts from a dozen to a score or more of different sources. This firm is only one of several distributors in the field, some of them as large or larger, each of which is a sales outlet for a considerable number of small and larger industries. All this is in one relatively small industrial area. A somewhat similar story can be told of any one of various other fields. Many possible industries call for advanced, specialized training, but others are open to persons of no more than high school education who have good judgment and sustained interest.

As the field for small industry closes in some directions through the advancement of technology, it opens in others through that same technology. So long as the dynamic character of our economy remains there will constantly be cases of obsolescence among existing industries, and constant opportunity for the pioneer. Small, independent industries are needed as laboratories and experiment stations in American economic life.

The "free enterprise system" is evolving into something very different from, and better than, what orthodox capitalism was a generation or two ago, and into something very different and more promising than capitalism today in Western Europe. Yet it still has a long way to go before it will be free from undesirable traits inherited from feudalism, and from European social and economic custom. Also, big business, like big government, big labor unions or big religious organization, tends to lose flexibility and pioneering spirit. Small business, with its greater freedom to adjust and explore, can try out new ideas and attitudes which it would be rash for big business to consider until they have been well proved. Even should the average big business be found more progressive than most little business, the occasional little undertaking which is even more ably led in a pioneering spirit, and perhaps with more than usual social sensitivity, can set better examples and demonstrate the feasibility of new attitudes and methods which can then be copied by both big and little business.

Occasionally a vigorous and creative-minded man not only develops a new invention or a new method, but may have more than ordinary exacting ethical standards and a whole new pattern of attitude and action in industry which he believes in and wants to try out. The pattern in his mind may include ways of dealing with production, marketing, public relations, employment, financing and advertising. That is, he may have an over-all life philosophy and attitude which he wishes to express. A small business of his own makes it possible for him to pioneer. In big business occasionally a branch manager is given wide freedom to work out his entire pattern of ideas, but usually a big corporation has its over-all policy which controls. That more small businessmen have not pioneered in the application of business and social ethics and purposes is a reflection on the individual, social and religious climate of America. Yet, what has been done is significant.

THE MAZZOLINI ART BRONZE FOUNDRY   *Photo by Dave Lutes*

Chapter III

THE IMPORTANCE OF LITTLE INDUSTRIES
TO SMALL COMMUNITIES

A major count against centralization of industry is one which it shares with modern life in general--the destruction of our indigenous small communities. Our country has a large stake in these small, primary groups. Throughout human history, and for a long period before that, the small community has been the chief means for transmitting such basic cultural traits as good will, neighborliness and mutual confidence, without which no society can thrive. Throughout the ages most men have lived in such social groups, and we have no records of any society or of any nation long surviving their general decay. During the past century England has become dominantly urban. The apparent progressive decline of present day British life, as indicated by Rountree and Lavers in *English Life and Leisure**, and in the not too conclusive reports of the declining "intelligence quotients" of British people made by leading British psychologists, suggest that modern peoples have achieved no immunity in this regard.

Unless there are reasonable chances for making their livings near home, young people will leave for the city, and with their leaving the home town loses some of its vigor and attractiveness. Nor is it enough that there is a chance to make a living near home. Occupational aptitudes and interests vary widely. Any community with a single economic base, whether it be factory, farming, mining, lumbering, fishing, quarrying, railroading or caring for vacationers, does not offer sufficient range for its young people. Only a minor part of them may be interested in the single local opportunity. If the communities of a region are monotonously alike in their employment opportunities, as sometimes is the case in a farming region, the young people will go where there is greater choice. A young person should not be driven to start another store or filling station, when there are already enough, in order to escape from the one dominant industry and yet remain in the home community. If the home town offers wide occupational choice, and especially if the towns of a locality have considerable variety in their economic activities, young men and women may find at home the work they

---

*Longmans Green and Company, London and New York, 1951.

THE ANTIOCH TOWERS, SEEN OVER GLEN HELEN FOREST

want, or their movements may largely be back and forth among the towns of the area, and the life and vigor of the region may be well maintained.

Small independent industries can share the life of the community more fully than can big business, even when it is decentralized. With local plants of decentralized big business, policy usually is made at a distance and the local community tends to become the ward of its destiny makers, whom it seldom if ever sees, and cannot know. In the evolution of big company policy a local plant may be abandoned or moved, leaving the community without an economic base. Where a plant is owned in the community the chance is greater that local interests will have consideration. In the locally owned small industry there tends to be less moving about of personnel, and more people may dare to own their own homes. Thus workers and their families more often get their roots in the home environment, and can help in developing the personality and quality of the community.

The small, independent business man, especially the industrialist whose market is widespread, often dares to speak his mind on public matters, whereas the local representative of non-resident ownership usually must reflect company policy. The greater number of competent, experienced, independent persons who share in the making of public policy, the sounder will be our democracy.

The wide distribution of population, and the continuity of vigorous small community life are so vital to our national well-being that they may well be promoted by public policy, even at the loss of some economic efficiency. It is in the interest of adequate and varied opportunities for the young men and women of our small communities that we are interested in small industries for small towns.

However, it would be unrealistic to ignore the possible values of decentralized large industries. With good social planning they need not mean the subjugation of a community to the status of a ward. It is becoming common for both locally owned industry, and for branches of large corporations, to locate, not in a small town but in the open country, within reach of several small towns or near a fairly densely settled area. Ten or twenty miles is not too far to go to work in the open country where roads are not crowded. In many parts of rural America today there are locally owned or decentralized industries scattered about so that a person living in any small town thereabouts has the choice of half a dozen different firms to work for. The working members of a neighborhood may start out in the morning in half a dozen different directions. With an eight-hour day and a five-day week these workers can still spend enough time with their families and in their communities to have good family and community life. Such advantages partly overcome the undesirable features of branch factories of large corporations.

The distribution of small industries in small communities over the country is very uneven. About ten years ago, in the process of writing a book on the subject, I traveled by auto over many parts of the country. Sometimes in a stretch of 100 miles or more, passing through numerous small towns, I would not find a single small industry in operation. In other sections, as in Lancaster County, Pennsylvania, and in parts of Massachusetts, Delaware and Vermont, and even in parts of Kansas and Nebraska, one would come upon them in most little villages, and sometimes along country roads.

There appeared to be no difference in human quality which would account for such diversity. Neither would proximity to industrial centers fully explain it. The chief reason seemed to be social custom and the imitativeness of people. An illustration of how this may work is provided by a situation in the southeast corner of North Carolina. A shirtwaist factory worker in Newark, New Jersey, was persuaded through advertising to buy 15 acres of land locally considered nearly worthless. He was a Hollander, knew bulbs, and began raising and selling them and cut flowers. Now 60 or 70 people in the neighborhood are doing the same, and sales of cut flowers, shipped north, amount to about $1,000,000 dollars a year. Sheer creativeness is rare, whereas the impulse to imitate is widespread.

In some places old craftsmanship persists under the shadow of the new technology. Holmes County, Ohio, south of Cleveland, is such a case. It is largely settled by the Amish and Mennonites. Here we find a great variety of little industries, mostly of the old craftsman type.

There is much room for research, pioneering and experimenting in working out the future of the small community in America. Our life is so varied in its interactions that no one pattern can monopolize the field. The small industry, preferably locally owned, has possibilities deserving increased attention.

BIRCH BROOK IN GLEN HELEN

Chapter IV

THE VILLAGE OF YELLOW SPRINGS
AND WHY INDUSTRIES LOCATED THERE

A glimpse of Yellow Springs will help to an understanding of its industries. In general appearance the village is reminiscent of New England. Located in southwestern Ohio, 20 miles east of Dayton, 10 miles south of Springfield, 60 miles north of Cincinnati and the same distance west of Columbus, it has a population, not counting college students, of about 2500. In 1921, when the rejuvenation of Antioch College was begun, it was an agricultural community of about 1300, a considerable part of its population composed of elderly retired farm people. With the revival of Antioch College, local property rose in value, and the village was no longer so frequently chosen as a retiring place by farmers.

In 1921, when the new Antioch program was begun, there was almost no industrial activity in the village. An ancient sawmill, a nearly defunct canning plant, a grain elevator, and a nursery which propagated evergreens from cuttings, with a combined total of perhaps 20 employees, supplied the only opportunities for industrial occupation in the village.

Antioch College

Antioch College was opened in 1853 with Horace Mann as first president. After his death in 1859 it had a long succession of difficulties. In 1920, just before the new program was undertaken, the total annual budget of the institution was less than $15,000, there were about 60 students, about two-thirds of them of high school grade. The buildings were much as they had been in 1853, except that they were in extreme disrepair. There was no plumbing in any of them.

The new Antioch program was initiated in the fall of 1921. During the first three years Mr. C.F. Kettering contributed $40,000 and loaned $300,000. This helped in the rehabilitation of the buildings and in getting the program started. After that, the college had no assured source of support. Repeatedly there was not money enough in sight to keep going for more than one or two months. The rapid growth of the college in the succeeding years, until the annual budget is 100 times as large and the college student body 50 times as large as in 1920, has had its effect on the village.

In the process of reorganization one central policy was consciously and definitely kept in mind which has influenced developments in the village. It was that education should concern itself, not with any one or a few phases of living, but with the whole of personality and of life. Every student should have both a liberal and a practical education. His liberal education should not be confined to any segment of culture, such as the humanities or science. Students specializing in the humanities were required to have courses in mathematics, physics, chemistry, geology, biology and psychology, while those specializing in natural sciences were required to take courses in literature, philosophy, and the social sciences. Because one must learn from life as well as from books, a program of alternating work and study was made a part of the new plan.

During the reorganization it was hoped that small industries might be developed adjacent to the college. They might be useful in supplying work experience and income to students on the work-and-study program, as a laboratory for instruction in business administration, to add to the income of the college, and to add to the range of occupations available to the young people of the village, so that they would not need to leave Yellow Springs in order to make a living.

Because of the extreme financial stress under which the new program was initiated, and with many elements of educational methods to master, it was several years before more than brief and hurried attention could be given to stimulating new industries. Their nurturing was never more than a marginal activity in a very strenuous program. Worst of all, there was not time and money available for a thorough search for men who combined industrial competence and experience with interest in education, awareness of social values, and a spirit of adventure which would lead them to take risks for new patterns of economic life. That search proved more difficult and baffling than securing good teachers. Industrial competence is commonly acquired along with deep indoctrination in the prevailing patterns of industry. Some industrial policies that are now widely accepted were then looked upon as visionary.

What was wanted was not simply to introduce students to industrial life as it is. They would get such introduction in their part-time outside jobs. It was hoped that while developing practical business competence they might be infected with a desire to adventure in creating new and better patterns of industrial policy. Sometimes it seemed that we had largely failed in this aim; yet when we see the integrity as to product and customer relations, and the progressive industrial relations attitudes of various Yellow Springs industries, discouragement with the outcome seems not to be appropriate. Many Antioch graduates with businesses of their own display an unusual range of interest in human relations in industry. In Yellow Springs this has expressed itself in employee ownership, employee representation on boards of directors and in policy making, profit sharing, absence of race discrimination in employment, vacations with pay, and in general in the treatment of employees as responsible associates rather than as industrial servants. This pioneering has not followed any single pattern. Some plants are fully unionized with full cooperation of the management. In others employees have freely chosen to be without unions, preferring the free play of relationships of mutual confidence and cooperation rather than the sometimes rather rigid conditions which often result from formal collective bargaining. Altogether, a number of the village industries have been something of an experimental laboratory in human relations in industry.

Antioch Associated Activities

With its concern for all-round living, including both practical and cultural life, and research as well as study, Antioch has incubated or sponsored or welcomed a variety of activities which are not industries, often not economic projects, but which add variety to the community and thereby to its attractiveness as a place to live and work. Mention of some of these may throw light on why young people wishing to establish small industries may be drawn to Yellow Springs.

KETTERING PHOTOSYNTHESIS RESEARCH. Because of interest in research at Antioch and of the exceptional ability of Dr. O.N. Inman of the Biology Department, C.F. Kettering chose the college as the location for long range research work in photosynthesis--the process by which plants use sunlight to produce starch, sugar and other carbohydrates. This has been carried on for more than 20 years with a staff of scientists. As this project has developed, Mr. Kettering has assigned various related problems to a considerable number of research workers in several institutions. Now it has been decided to bring a large part of the work together at a single research center. To make this possible Mr. Kettering is beginning the construction of a half million dollar research building on the Antioch campus.

THE FELS RESEARCH INSTITUTE FOR THE STUDY OF HUMAN DEVELOPMENT. More than 40 years ago I became interested in over-all study of the factors of child development to throw light on environmental and inborn factors in human inheritance. For 20 years I sought unsuccessfully to interest someone in financing such a project. Most biological research dealt with specific, limited problems. Biologists insisted than an over-all study of the factors of child development would be too general to be scientific. Then Samuel Fels of Philadelphia took an interest. He said the biologists' misgivings did not trouble him, and he made it possible to initiate such an undertaking. Dr. Lester Sontag was put in charge, and he has been directing the project since 1929. Beginning with but one helper in a three-room cottage, he has seen the project grow until now it is housed in a very well equipped million-dollar plant, with a staff of about 30 scientific workers and assistants. Such persons in a community add to the variety of cultural resources and associations.

OTHER RESEARCH PROJECTS. Other research projects such as those in the interest of the National Cash Register Company and of the U.S. Army Signal Corps, and the U.S. Airforce, as well as "pure research" financed by the Research Foundation, add somewhat to sources of livelihood and to the number of the people in the village who have cultural interests.

GLEN HELEN. This tract of about 950 acres, including some primeval forest with rock cliffs, brooks and tumbling waters, was given to the college in 1928 to 1930 by Hugh T. Birch, of the class of 1869. While the major part is kept as a wilderness preserve, especially for the students, there is room also for a forest laboratory, a school forest for Yellow Springs children, and a modern demonstration farm. Under the direction of Kenneth Hunt it has become a meeting place for foresters, nature study groups, biologists, geologists and farm management people, thus adding to the cultural resources of the community. It also provides a beautiful "green-belt" along the east side of the village.

All over America there are beautiful river banks being used for dumping grounds, fine woods being cut for the little lumber they yield, and other rare bits of nature adjoining small communities being desecrated, and sometimes permanently ruined, because no one realizes what their preservation would mean to the life of the community.

THE YELLOW SPRINGS AREA THEATER. With the beginning of the new Antioch program during 1921 Mrs. Morgan initiated a weekly dramatics reading group in our home. It grew through the years into an active dramatics movement which made great headway under the dynamic and able direction of Mrs. Imogene Putnam, who made it a vital part of the community life. She was succeeded by Basil Pillard, and he, after a few years, by Paul Treichler and Arthur Lithgow, both well trained in the theater, Treichler at the Yale School of Drama and Lithgow at Cornell. Since 1947 this group has been known as the Yellow Springs Area Theater. The staff is made up of college and town people, and of persons from nearby cities. A program of plays is presented at Yellow Springs each winter, and during the summer the cast sometimes goes on the road. During the local programs the audiences include people from Springfield, Dayton, Columbus and Cincinnati.

In 1952 the Area Theater presented a summer of "Shakespeare Under the Stars," a complete program of the historical dramas, the first time the entire group had been given in sequence in America. The series drew many visitors from Ohio cities and from other parts of the country, and were well reported in the national press.

The theater has become a well-established element in Yellow Springs life. When Morris Bean and Company moved to its new plant in 1951 the Area Theater took over the old foundry building which, as Brooks Atkinson wrote after visiting it, is space fortunately free from those rigidities which most theater architects impose as a result of their ideas as to what a theater should be like.

Why Are Small Industries Attracted to the Village

When one notes the extremely varied types of industry in Yellow Springs, where in 1921 there was practically none, he may wonder just what is the common element which has attracted them, or caused their growth. Not a single one of the dozen started there came as the result of the Chamber of Commerce type of activity of finding a firm seeking a location and persuading it to come. In no case has there been the customary incentive of a free building site or remission of taxes. Yellow Springs is in a part of the country where there is much expression of personal initiative, and so no wholly local explanation of its industries can be entirely adequate: yet the unusual variety in those that have developed during the past 25 years is in some degree a local phenomenon.

One factor which has influenced men to choose Yellow Springs is the friendly neighborliness which has marked the village for a century past. Sometimes we forget how much we owe to the spirit which has survived from earlier days of simpler living. Yet that is not a complete explanation, for there are many small towns with similar friendly spirit which have no local industries.

A possible explanation is that small industries like to locate in a college town. Yet there are hundreds of small American towns with colleges, but which have few if any industries.

Some industries started by old Yellow Springs families have had little or no direct association with the college. Yet no doubt in the recent past Antioch has been a factor in the situation. The chance to get questions answered in the science laboratories, access to the College library, opportunity to get advice from scientists, accountants, labor relations men, business admmnistration specialists, or economists--all this helps. Ability to get pairs of part-time ("co-op") students as employees, with the prospect that some of them will remain as permanent employees or as associates after graduation, no doubt has been a factor. In some of these local industries and services the executives and supervisory staff members are largely Antioch graduates. The periods of working experience gave to some students a sense of self-reliance so that they were not afraid to undertake things "on their own." On the other hand, these practical entrepreneurs had taken courses in history, government, industrial relations and sociology. Each one of them had had at least one course in the fine arts. They were not divided between "practical" persons and "cultured" persons, but were a union of both. When Yellow Springs puts on its annual "Arts Show" the variety of amateur production is surprising.

Yellow Springs is one of the smaller American communities to have adopted the Council-Manager form of municipal government, which represents a marked advance in public administration. However, this form of local government was not adopted until after nearly all the town's little industries and other economic ventures were well underway.

By and large, what has attracted outsiders to start their
little industries in the village is its general atmosphere.
They like the village. They like its variety of outlooks and
interests, its spirit of adventure and inquiry. They like
the old-time neighborly friendliness, which the Community
Council and other groups are trying to keep alive. Many a
person in business for himself wishes to be more than a manufacturer. He would like to be an intelligent and interested
human being as well. When he finds a community where a considerable number of people have similar goals he and his
wife are inclined to want to go there.

A Sound Basis for Community Development

For persons considering ways to increase industrial life
in their communities one general inference might be drawn
from the Yellow Springs experience. It is that "man does not
live by bread alone." If we could get a true rendering of
the rest of that Biblical passage it might be to the effect
that man lives by everything that concerns his life and experience. A person considering spending his life in a community is concerned with health conditions, education, cultural and intellectual life, space for children's play and
recreation, variety of associations and experience, the
character of the people in ethical and spiritual standards,
and with opportunities to make a living in ways he can enjoy
and respect.

If this is true, then the securing and developing of community industries is not just a matter of getting factories
located and under way. It means building a total life and
environment in which interesting and competent people will
like to participate. It means also achieving human relations
in industry such that intelligent and self-respecting employees can feel that they are not just cogs in a machine, but
are associates in an undertaking which they can hold in high
regard.

That will not be the work of a year, or even of a single
decade. If one's life interest is in building a good and
enduring community in all of its varied aspects, then the
creation of an economic base for community living will have
an important place in one's endeavors; but that interest in
economic development will be part of a total undertaking,
and not an isolated project.

Beginnings may be very simple. If there is a core of
sound, honest and friendly people and a persistent spark of
inquiry and adventure, then all the rest can be added in
course of time, though the time may seem long and the progress slow. As I observe the small final residue of human
value in many spectacular undertakings, I come increasingly
to the opinion that to spend one's years in helping a community to get a deep and strong foundation for a good and
full total way of living is one of the best uses one can
make of his years.

Characteristic Yellow Springs Undertakings

There are in the community a number of institutions which
can be found in almost any American village of two or three
thousand people. These include stores, service stations,
churches, luncheon clubs, parent-teachers' associations, boy
and girl scout troops, American Legion posts, and a number
of others. Yellow Springs has its full share of these, and
they need no description. In addition some communities have
undertakings more or less of their own creation, which give
them individuality. Yellow Springs has its share of these.

THE COMMUNITY COUNCIL. For ten years past this has been
a sort of clearing house for community interests. Each civic
organization in the village appoints a representative, and
these together make up the council. Since such organizations
cut across all political, social and economic lines, a rep-
representative body results. In case any class or group of
people is not represented, the council may "co-opt" a few
members to make its body more fully representative. A few
persons with special skills or experience such as a physician
or an educator, may also be co-opted as members. The civic
groups which elect representatives include churches, luncheon clubs, parent-teachers' association, League of Women
Voters, American Legion, the local high school, the College
and a few others.

The Community Council directs the local Community Chest
and allocates funds to such activities as the Boy Scouts and
Girl Scouts, the Library Association, 4-H Clubs, the Yellow
Springs Youth Council, the Community Nursery School, and the
Community Center building. A community calendar is developed
covering all meetings and happenings in the village. This is
published weekly in the local paper. Where no other organization is ready to undertake some needed service, the Community Council may do so itself.

THE MILLS HOUSE. This is the original old "Mansion House" built by the founder of the village more than a century ago. It is a three-story structure of about 20 large rooms. Acquired by the school district and operated by the Community Council, it serves as a center for community activities and houses the Community Nursery School.

CHILDREN'S DAY CAMP. Through the operation of a "Goods Exchange" to which villagers contribute their surplus belongings for sale at moderate prices, funds are accumulated for operating a summer day camp for children five to ten years old. Twice a week the children get a swim in a nearby pool. The Goods Exchange and the day camp are largely the work of one woman, Mrs. C.S. Adams.

WEEKLY MUSIC CONCERT. One evening each week during the summer an outdoor musical concert is provided. The talent comes from the village and surrounding towns.

THE YELLOW SPRINGS ARTS ASSOCIATION gives expression to artistic interests in many fields. The annual Community Arts Festival will have over a hundred local exhibitors in oils, drawings, water colors, tempera, sculpture, masks, stained glass, ceramics, metal, wood, jewelry, crafts, architecture and photography.

THE YOUTH COUNCIL provides guidance, recreation, vocational training, and small scholarships, and is one of the larger of the community programs.

THE LOCAL BANK, like the stores and service stations, is one of those small community institutions which might be taken for granted without mention as being characteristic of a particular community. Yet the local bank can be a distinctive institution, and in Yellow Springs it is. Russell Stewart, the present president, is son of the founder, and a graduate of Antioch College. The bank's loans to local small industries have been based as much or more upon intimate acquaintance with the persons involved than upon the collateral security provided by borrowers. Some of the little industries might not have started, or might not have survived, but for that discriminating, friendly help. Where large loans have been sought from big city banks, Russell Stewart's judgment of the local situation has been a factor in the decisions reached.

Two organizations of more than local activity have their headquarters in Yellow Springs. One of these is the American Humanist Association, which publishes a bi-monthly magazine, *The Humanist*. The other is Community Service, Inc., an organization whose activities are national and international. It was incorporated in 1940 as a non-profit organization to supply information and services to small communities. Throughout its field of activity, by means of publications, consultations, conferences and correspondence, it undertakes to increase awareness of community values, possibilities in community economic life, education for community life and possibilities for community health, cultural interests, recreation, adventure and pioneering. It publishes a quarterly magazine, *Community Service News*.

These activities are mentioned to emphasize the fact that it is no one quality or resource which makes a community a desirable location for small industry, but the general flavor and character of the place. Industry is made up primarily of people, and these people have a range of needs and interests. The more fully they are satisfied, the more will that community be an acceptable location for industry.

The descriptions of Yellow Springs small industries which follow will give an idea of their variety and of the varied ways in which they originated.

Chapter V

INDUSTRIES IN METAL AND RUBBER

1. The Antioch Foundry--Morris Bean and Company

With about 250 men at work, Morris Bean and Company is the largest Yellow Springs employer. In the description of the beginnings of the Art Bronze Foundry of Amos Mazzolini there is an account of the origin of that undertaking and of the beginning of research in aluminum casting. As Morris Bean worked in the Bronze foundry, developing possibilities in the laboratory and then trying them out in the foundry located in a remodelled dairy barn, he departed from the methods of lost wax casting and created a new method for casting aluminum, now known in industry as "the Antioch process." With this accomplished he came to see greater promise in aluminum than in bronze.

However, progress seemed very slow. When five or six years had passed and it was still only a struggling undertaking, experienced men who counselled me on business matters strongly advised dropping the venture. "There is a sound industrial opinion," one of them said, "that if an undertaking does not show definite progress in five years it is time to drop it and try something else." I refused to take that course, partly, perhaps, because of unwillingness to admit defeat, but partly from a feeling that Amos Mazzolini and Morris Bean, each in his own way, was not just fumbling blindly, but was working with an element of design and of orderly progress. I felt that the essential period of gestation for a creative undertaking cannot be estimated accurately as it can be in breeding cattle.

The foundry continued with the help of a very little money gathered here and there. When I left to go to the T.V.A. my successor, Algo D. Henderson, gave it more trained financial counsel. Without that help it probably would not have survived. After Mazzolini and Bean separated, Mazzolini working with art bronze and Bean with aluminum, gradually Morris Bean's thoroughgoing, original analysis of the problems of aluminum casting began to bear fruit. His process filled a place which nothing else did. Morris Bean's wife, Xarifa, who was also Antioch trained, worked with him in research and became a major factor in the development. Morris' mother and sisters helped by looking after the four children during working hours.

In 1952 Antioch conferred on Morris and Xarifa Bean jointly the honorary degrees of LL.D. in recognition of their common achievement.

One of the Beans' first striking successes was in making molds in which automobile tire treads are cured. Through cooperative research with the Goodyear Rubber Company there was demonstration that the foundry could make aluminum molds for considerable less than steel molds were costing, and the Rubber Company gave a trial order. Within a few years the Antioch foundry was making most of such molds for Goodyear, Goodrich, Firestone and the United States Rubber Company. The foundry had moved from an old barn to a better one, but still was located in a remodelled dairy barn.

Another early product was an aluminum rotor used in General Motor's new Diesel engines, then coming onto the market in quantity. This requires especially smooth and regular surfaces on inside spiral passages that cannot be machined. For a few years all such rotors used by General Motors were made in the Antioch Foundry.

With the advent of the Second World War the Army and the Navy called for Antioch Foundry products on a scale far beyond its resources to produce. As a result the foundry and its processes were sold to General Motors, the right being retained for the Antioch group to enter into business for itself with the process after five years. General Motors then built a larger foundry on the Antioch campus adjoining the dairy barn. Morris Bean operated this for five years. General Motors also built a new plant at Muncie, Indiana, for making Diesel engine rotors by the Antioch Process. Men were sent by General Motors to learn the process in the Antioch foundry, and men from that foundry were also sent to Muncie to train workmen in the process.

At the end of five years the Antioch group repurchased the Yellow Springs foundry after friendly negotiations during which General Motors showed its appreciation of the value of small, independent, highly skilled industry, and sold the plant on reasonable terms. At this point the College disposed of the control to Morris Bean, and it has been operated as an independent industry since that time. The name was changed from the Antioch Foundry to Morris Bean and Company. Antioch College retains some stock in the company from which it receives a substantial income.

INTRICATE PRECISION CASTING--MORRIS BEAN & CO. FOUNDRY

As at present constituted, Morris Bean and Company is a
locally owned corporation, most of its stockholders and most
of its directors being employees of the company. The vigorous, young directing staff is mostly made up of graduates of
Antioch College. The company pays wages about equal to those
of General Motors and has a profit sharing plan and vacations
with pay. Under General Motors it was unionized. When it was
repurchased the employees decided that they preferred the
free give-and-take of friendly personal relations and withdrew from the union, though the union sent in workers and
made an intense campaign to bring about a contrary result.
The employees have free access to the books of the company,
except in case of confidential government business, and are
kept informed of the state of the business, unfilled orders,
etc. The success of the company is due in no small degree to
high employee morale and the high level of mutual confidence.

As business continued to expand, the plant built on the
Antioch campus by General Motors became entirely inadequate.
In 1950 the company began the erection of a new building
about a mile and a half from the village. This plant, which

it now occupies, and the necessary new equipment, cost about $850,000. Also an overflow plant at the nearby village of Cedarville has been put into operation on a new process for iron casting developed under the research direction of Mrs. Bean. Sales at present are at the rate of about $2,000,000 a year. Of the 250 men employed, most are from the village of Yellow Springs or from surrounding farms or villages. About half of them own stock in the company.

So far the company has done no advertising and has not used the services of sales representatives. Capital and management, like the employees, are mostly local products. As Morris Bean sometimes remarks, there are at least half a dozen persons without whose efforts the undertaking could not have survived. With the present competent and varied supervisory staff of young men it seems that the survival and growth of the company does not depend on any one or two or three persons. Seldom does an industry of its size have such a substantial body of young supervisors, any one of whom, if necessary, could assume general management.

A BAY OF THE MORRIS BEAN FOUNDRY

2. *The Antioch Industrial Research Laboratory*

While president of Antioch I continued to maintain an engineering practice which in various ways helped the college budget. In the late 1920's our engineering firm, the Dayton-Morgan Engineering Company, undertook a piece of engineering research and development for the Case, Pomeroy Company of New York, which was engaged in industrial research, development and operation. Walter S. Case, the president, was a trustee of Antioch College.

This development, directed by Barton M. Jones, then head of civil engineering at Antioch, was markedly successful and profitable. In appreciation Mr. Case suggested that his company set up a fund of $100,000 to maintain an industrial research project at Antioch for the mutual benefit of the college and his company. Case, Pomeroy suggested projects and proposed persons for employment who were considered to be able research men.

Two projects, one for the chemical reduction of beryllium and another for a radio recording instrument for distant rainfall and river gauge stations, were not successfully concluded by the men sent by Case, Pomeroy to work at them.

The third man sent by Case, Pomeroy was Sergius Vernet. He was interested in a new principle of thermostat design. He worked with intelligence, persistence and practical judgment, with results that are described under the account of the Vernay Laboratories.

In 1933 I became chairman of the T.V.A. and my intimate association with Antioch came to a close. With the death of Walter Case the relations between Case, Pomeroy and the college changed. The remaining funds were withdrawn by the company, and thus ended the Antioch Industrial Research Project, except as the parties retained interest in Mr. Vernet's work. Through that connection Case, Pomeroy recovered its investment in the research project, with a margin of profit.

3. *The Vernay Laboratories Company*

When the Antioch Industrial Research project was liquidated, Sergius Vernet remained at Antioch, continuing the work he had begun under that project. Interest in it was divided between Vernet and Case, Pomeroy, with Antioch College retaining certain interest in the form of royalties.

Working in the Antioch Science Building, and using Antioch "co-op" students as assistants, Mr. Vernet continued the development of his thermostat. It was based on the fact that some crystalline substances expand and exert pressure when they freeze and crystallize, while others expand when they melt and lose their crystalline structure. A common example is that water in freezing will expand and exert such great pressure that it will burst pipes. Vernet's idea was to make such pressure do useful work. Combinations of different substances can be made that will expand or contract at almost any desired temperature.

The general idea was simple enough, but efforts to apply it met with a vast amount of difficulty. It was Mr. Vernet's imagination in seeing possible solutions and his practical competence in working them out that were the basis of his success. As his thermostat became practicable he licensed its manufacture, but continued his research on its improvement and upon its adaptation to many uses. How successful he has been is indicated by the fact that today nearly every household washing machine, airplane, and army tank uses one or more of the thermostats, as do all Ford automobiles and one or two other makes of car.

When there was no longer room in the college science building for his work, Vernet built a small, modern industrial plant a block away. With the rapid growth of the business he has enlarged the plant seven times in four years.

While he licensed the manufacture of his thermostats to a firm in Detroit, he continues to make the expansion material which is used in all of them. This in itself is an interesting small industry for the village. Also Vernet's thermostats demand certain precision hard rubber parts which he could not find in satisfactory quality in the market. Rather than have his thermostats faulty Vernet undertook through a program of research to develop processes for making these parts at his Yellow Springs plant. He went at this with the same intelligent thoroughness that had characterized the development of his thermostat. When he had done this to his own satisfaction he found that he had, in fact, created a new type of industrial product--precision hard rubber moldings. American industry seemed to have been waiting for just such a product, and demand came from many directions. Soon his rubber moldings outstripped the thermostat business. It

is that development which has called for the frequent en-
largements of his plant. At present, of the company's 130
employees about 20 are research workers. The company makes
materials and parts for about 800,000 thermostats a month.
In the field of precision rubber moldings it makes nearly
300 different products.   808015

Vernet is now doing a business of $1,500,000 a year. Of
this, about $100,000 comes from research services rendered
to industry, $200,000 from the making of thermostat parts
and materials, and $1,200,000 from the manufacture of preci-
sion rubber moldings. Because of the continued growth of the
industry, Mr. Vernet plans to construct an entirely new plant
for manufacture, and to use the present buildings just for
research service to industry generally, for the development
of new products.

Rights in the thermostat development are separately organized as "Vernay Patents." Antioch College has recently acquired the Case, Pomeroy rights, and its income from this
source is equal to that on a million-dollar endowment.

Vernet's industrial relations policies are on a high level.
Among his one hundred and thirty employees there is no race
discrimination. Two of his most skillful machinists are
Negroes, one of whom trained as an apprentice in the plant's
training program. There have been no problems arising from
the fact that some of the supervisors are Negroes.

The plant is unionized. When the C.I.O. organized a new
union in an effort to break free from communist domination,
according to Mr. Vernet the Vernay local voted unanimously to
go with the new C.I.O. union. Wages are on a level with those
in progressive industrial plants in Dayton or Detroit. Weekly
earnings for the time worked in 1951 by hourly wage workers
averaged about $91. The company has profit sharing, pensions,
and vacations with pay. Mr. Vernet is proud of the fact that
although there are no paternalistic housing projects, the
employees do save money and build substantial homes. This is
true regardless of race or color. The illustrated home of a
Negro worker is similar to numerous others which might have
been pictured.

Mr. Vernet feels that the presence of Antioch College has
been a very desirable element in his undertaking. It afford-

ed a good starting place for his project. Antioch part-time (co-op) students furnished a considerable part of his early working force. At present there are nine "co-op" students employed, five in research and four in production. Several of the present staff members began as Antioch "co-op" students before becoming full-time employees. Two faculty members are working on the staff part time to supplement their income, and others work there during vacations. Antioch science faculty members provide a highly valued source of counsel. One of the directors of the company, in charge of research, continues to act as head of the Antioch chemistry department. The chief engineer and production manager also is an Antioch graduate, and so are the chief chemist and the quality control chemist, and several research chemists. The laboratories of the college are useful in the solution of special problems, student workers continue to be available, and the general college atmosphere makes the village a desirable location for the industry.

VIEW IN THE VERNAY LABORATORIES CO. PLANT

Chapter VI

INDUSTRIES SERVING RESEARCH

1. *The Yellow Springs Instrument Company*

The Yellow Springs Instrument Company began as a local development to meet local needs. The Fels Institute for the Study of Child Development, which had grown up through twenty years in association with Antioch College, from time to time needed instruments for measuring and recording heart action, blood pressure, skin temperature, and other bodily conditions, with greater accuracy than was feasible with existing devices. An Antioch student, John Benedict, made the production of such equipment his "co-op" job, being counseled by Hardy Trolander, who graduated from Antioch in 1947, and remained as a college instructor in physics the following year. David Jones, after graduating from Antioch in 1943, spent several years in military service, part of the time being stationed in New York City, after which he did graduate work at Ohio State University. In 1948 he returned to Yellow Springs, and with Trolander launched the new business. A little later Dave Case, Antioch 1943, and John Benedict, Antioch 1948, became members of the firm.

At first they made equipment for various Antioch laboratories and for the Fels Institute. Then some of their developments proved to be useful elsewhere. Among those for which a larger market has been found are a dielectric constant meter, and a camera timer which will control the length of exposure to within five one-thousandths of a second. Another somewhat similar precise camera timer is being built for Boeing Aircraft. Other products in production or in process are an electronic stop watch accurate within one ten-thousandth of a second, an instrument for measuring the rate of blood flow, a multichannel amplifier for very weak signals, and a wide range sound-level meter. Some of these developments have required the overcoming of very stubborn technical difficulties. Some are for individual special orders, as for Wright Field aircraft research. Others are in routine production for college and industrial laboratories.

At first the firm rented two rooms in the Antioch Science Building. As the market developed, these became inadequate and they rented a part of the new Antioch engineering building while their own new plant was under construction a short distance south of the village. This they now occupy. In addition to the four members of the firm there are a full-time foreman, a full-time engineer (Antioch graduate of 1949) and three or four other employees. From time to time Antioch part time "co-op" science or engineering students are used. Professor D.A. Magruder of the college advises on financial matters, while Fred Hooven, Antioch faculty member and engineering consultant, advises on technical problems and serves as a member of the board of directors.

Yellow Springs
Instrument Co.

SIX CHANNEL SOUND AMPLIFIER FOR STRAIN MEASUREMENTS

The firm has no sales organization. The members do not want to divide their attention between research and manufacture on the one hand and marketing on the other. Research and development projects are taken on directly from such organizations as the Atomic Energy Commission or Boeing Aircraft. Articles in routine production are marketed through a scientific instrument distributing firm. The company plans to keep away from mass production. They fear that the problems of large-scale manufacture might dull the keen edge of research. The policy is that when a product is developed for which there is a large potential demand it will be licensed to a production firm on a royalty basis.

It is the aim of the firm to meet its current operating costs by the manufacture of standard laboratory equipment on less than a mass-production basis. In this way they hope to

finance their research work. Some of their projects are long-
time undertakings. They believe that ten years is a reasonable period for developing them to a point at which the firm
will be well established. (The partners now range in age
from 29 to 32.)

I asked what the members of the firm thought of a village
such as Yellow Springs as a site for a technical industry
like theirs. They should know, for they have "been around."
Trolander grew up in Chicago, while Jones grew up in Yellow
Springs but worked for several years about New York City.
Benedict came from Hartford, Connecticut, and Case lived on
Staten Island. All of them in their part-time service on the
Antioch work-and-study program had worked in the New York
City area. Their conclusion is that for their business there
is absolutely no disadvantage in being located in the vil-
lage. They say that so long as they are not in the wilder-
ness, location is unimportant so far as economic factors are
concerned.

The markets for their products and the sources of their
materials and components are so widely scattered that wher-

STRAIN MEASURING
EQUIPMENT

NOSKER ENGINEERING PRODUCTS

ever they should be located they would be buying and selling outside the local area. The proximity to Dayton and Springfield is convenient. They believe that the quality of their work is better than it would be if they were located in a city. Trolander, for instance, having grown up in Chicago, having worked in various large cities while in military service, and having worked in New York City on a "co-op" job, and then having attended college in a village, came to the deliberate conclusion that he wanted to spend his life in a small town. Asked whether, having grown up in Chicago, he did not feel a pull back to the city, he replied, "Lord, no! Any feeling is of repulsion." After living in Yellow Springs he has the feeling that all may not be well in Chicago. The friendly neighborliness and the simplicity and the absence of social competition are both pleasant and economical of time and energy. Their new building, in the open country a mile from the village, is in a pleasant setting for undisturbed work.

2. The Nosker Engineering Products Co.

For many years the Nosker family have lived in Yellow Springs where the father taught biology at Antioch, and also helped to initiate the raising of hybrid corn seed. He died when Robert and Lowell were young, leaving the family in limited circumstances. Then Robert had a very serious illness which incapacitated him for years. Due to these circumstances neither of the Nosker boys finished college. In fact, Robert has only a high school education. An older brother, Paul, was further along when family difficulties came, and made physics his major field at Antioch.

While Paul was working as a physicist at the Wright Field aeronautical laboratories he observed serious limitations in some of the laboratory equipment he had to use. He talked these difficulties over with his younger brothers, who also had bents for physics and mechanics. The outcome was that Robert and Lowell decided to produce some equipment to overcome certain deficiencies. They started to work in an outbuilding back of the farm house in which they lived. (What would the small industries of Yellow Springs have done for starting-places without the various barns, sheds, cellars and attics which were left over from an agricultural era!)

Typical products of this little industry are the Nosker Strain Measuring Indicator and the Strain Recorder. The strain indicator is an electronic device for measuring strains in wood, metal and plastic structures. It is a complex technical assembly. The strain recorder is a device for recording the reading on this indicator. "As many as ten strain indicators may be connected to a single recorder, to give full automatic readings of as many as 480 channels at the rate of three channels per second."

This is about the smallest of Yellow Springs industries, most of the products being used in aeronautical research. The two brothers do all of the work themselves. Around their shop one sees a number of other projects in course of development, all of them, I believe, in the field of electronics.

3. The Velsey Co.: Granite Surface Plates

In many research laboratories and precision workshops it is necessary to have table tops that are uniformly flat with a high degree of precision. Practically always these were made of iron. In a curious way this need gave rise to a new industrial product and to another interesting small industry at Yellow Springs.

In 1942 Seth Velsey was a young sculptor in Dayton, Ohio. He worked in both wood and stone, and one of his carved wood figures had taken a first prize at the Paris International Exposition before the Second World War. Because he needed compressed air for stone carving he arranged to do some of his work in the Herman Stone Yard at Dayton, where compressed air was available. To help out his income he sometimes worked for the Herman Company at ornamental stone carving.

The son of the proprietor of the Herman Company decided to go into business for himself in running a machine shop for precision work, and he asked Velsey where he might find a precision iron plate. (They were scarce during the war.) Velsey replied jokingly that a man working in stone should be working on stone plates rather than iron. When Herman, Jr., remarked some time later that he thought Velsey's idea had promise, Velsey had forgotten his suggestion and did not know what was being referred to.

The two talked the subject over and decided to work it out together. Sculpture was "out" during the war, and another source of income was necessary. Iron precision plates have certain disadvantages. An iron plate tends to bulge when a piece of metal is dropped on it, or it may corrode or become magnetic. Also, steel was in short supply during the war. So far as they could find, stone had never been used as a base for precision instruments, except that an elderly Swiss told of seeing a stone used in a watchmaker's shop half a century before. It seems, therefore, that this was a new conception to these men, and not an adaptation of the printer's imposing stone.

They worked out the idea together, but decided to set up in business separately. Herman went to work with granite, whereas Velsey set out on a wide search of stone types to find one with just the characteristics he wanted. In this search he used an Antioch student for making laboratory tests, and so came into intimate touch with the College.

He settled upon a very hard, heavy, nearly black stone known as olivine diabase, which is commercially classified with the granites. It weighs two hundred pounds to the cubic foot as against one hundred sixty-five for granite, absorbs only three per cent as much water as granite when wet, and has other marked advantages. Having his proposed business thus "founded upon a rock," he laid plans for getting into production.

Velsey had a brother and sister living in a small town in Indiana, and from visiting them he came to feel that such a place to live had great advantages over a large city. Since Yellow Springs was the most desirable small town he knew, he decided to locate there. With the help of his friends he searched the town for a place to rent, but found none. So he purchased a property that was for sale, an old-fashioned home with a garden and fruit trees.

This is not the place to detail the problems Velsey met in developing this new industrial product. Sometimes a new industry turns out a crude product and gradually improves it through the years. Others are like Gutenberg, reputed inventor of printing, whose early work was so fine that after 500 years it remains a standard of quality. Velsey tried to do a nearly perfect job from the start. He studied the physical and chemical characteristics of his olivine diabase stone with suitable laboratory tests, and also learned the needs of research laboratories, and familiarized himself with the methods by which precision surfaces are produced.

The result of these preparations is the Velsey Olivine Diabase Surface Plates (known to the market as granite sur-

face plates). These are made in sizes up to six feet wide
and twelve feet long. The surface is made a true plane with
variations of not more than five one-hundred-thousandths
(.00005) of an inch. If desired for special purposes the
variations can be reduced to .00001 (one one-hundred-thou-
sandth) of an inch. Whereas an iron plate must be refinished
each year at a cost of several hundred dollars for a large
plate, Velsey's plates are guaranteed for ten years. If they
are damaged during that time he will refinish them without
charge except for transportation cost.

The result of this thoroughgoing preparation and careful
manufacture shows up in the market for the product. General
Motors uses them in four plants of the Chevrolet Division
and in the Allison, Aeroproducts, A.C. Spark Plug, Buick,
Cleveland Diesel, Delco Products and Frigidaire Divisions.
They are used also by Allis Chalmers, Army Air Forces at
Dayton and Detroit, Chrysler Corp., Cincinnati Milling Ma-
chine, Eastman Kodak, Thomas A. Edison, Inc., General
Electric (at ten different plants), International Harvester,
International Business Machines, Monsanto Chemical, National
Cash Register, U.S. Naval Observatory, Westinghouse, Western
Electric, and numerous smaller concerns.

Asked about the suitability of a village such as Yellow
Springs for a small industry like his, Mr. Velsey replied
that the chief disadvantage is in transportation. His product is very heavy, yet requires very careful handling to
prevent damage, especially for shipments to New York, New
England, or Canada. In a large city specialized transportation facilities would be more easily available. Otherwise he
found marked advantages in a village, and no disadvantages.
He expected difficulty in securing the quality of employees
he needs, but found no such difficulty. His present employees
tell him of friends and neighbors who would like to work for
him. Yellow Springs, he finds, is a desirable place in which
to live and to work. The great variety in the population,
including small industrialists, businessmen, artists, scientists, with a considerable sprinkling of men and women from
other countries, is stimulating. He knows of no other small
town so interesting to live in.

Velsey's project is an excellent illustration of the fact
that small industry is needed in American industrial life.
The great industries of the country call for his product,
yet the total business is so small that he and about a dozen

employees can supply the demand. What big corporation would want to set up a "Granite Surface Plates Division"? If one of them should do so, think of the trouble of getting the right man to run it, and of getting employees who would take the great pains needed, and who yet would be promoted by a rigid seniority rule, such as characterizes most labor-management contracts. And cannot Velsey take more satisfaction out of his work? His employees are his neighbors and friends. He himself is not just a production man. He is an artist, research man, inventor and man of cultural interests. He has freedom of action to express himself. He would rather sit in the shade of his own Rome Beauty apple tree and share the fruit with his neighbors than attend company staff meetings. Yet his work gives him contact with good minds. There are many such opportunities in America.

As physical, biological and psychological research expands to a billion dollar a year expenditure it inevitably must call for an unending variety of specialized equipment. The meeting of those exacting and highly specialized needs will continue to call for many small, independent industries.

Velsey Stone Surface Plates in Use in Buick Auto Plant

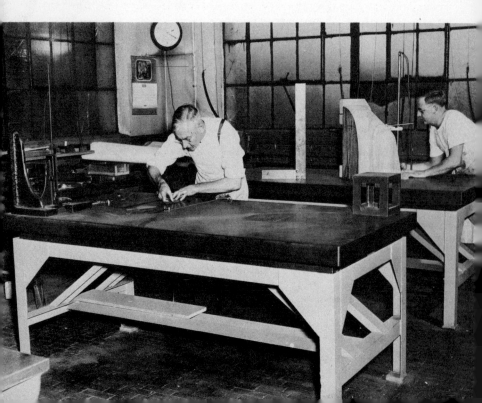

Chapter VII

PRINTING ESTABLISHMENTS

1. *The Antioch Bookplate Company*

Two Antioch part time (co-op) students, Walter Kahoe and Ernest Morgan, alternated in working in the William E. Rudge printing plant at Mount Vernon, a suburb of New York. One of the great printers of America, Bruce Rogers, then had his work shop in the Rudge plant, and the boys had occasional opportunity to talk to him and to get his advice. Each of them developed an attraction for the printer's art from which he never recovered.

It was while attending Antioch in the middle 1920's that they started a little business of making bookplates. Walter Kahoe, his interest ranging elsewhere, sold his share in the venture to his partner for $400. Walter had a variety of experiences before he became associated with the Lippincott Publishing Company, where he is now secretary of the Company and Vice President in charge of the medical books department, which has become one of the nation's largest medical publishing houses.

Ernest Morgan continued with bookplates. To get started in his little business he took time off from his studies and searched about the neighboring region for second hand printing equipment. He bought about $200 worth, which came within the limits of his savings. Then, instead of returning to his part time job he worked for himself while attending college.

To sell bookplates he "hitchhiked" through the midwest to get dealers, and then filled their orders in his hole-in-the wall print shop. During his first year his total sales were $300, his second year $600, the third year $1500; then, out of college and working full time, they increased more rapidly.

The business was an unfortunate choice in that it was inherently too small. Few businesses of the size had so many technical problems. Their solution might have related to issues on a much larger scale. Also, the making of bookplates had an attraction for artists, printers and manufacturers of greeting cards, and competition has been persistent. More than thirty persons or firms, from individual printers or artists to some of the largest greeting card

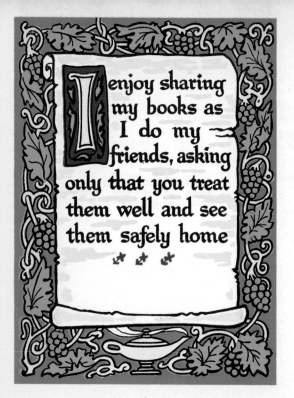

I enjoy sharing my books as I do my friends, asking only that you treat them well and see them safely home

Of the hundreds of Antioch Bookplate designs, the one shown here is among the more popular, about three million copies of this bookplate having been sold during the past ten years.

companies, have undertaken to compete in this little field. Practically all of these competitors were located in very large cities. As they have one by one given up the contest the Bookplate Company frequently has bought their plates and has added any of value to its own stock. But even though the company has won a near monopoly of its field, making perhaps 85% of all the bookplates produced in America, the business still amounts to only between $100,000 and $150,000 a year, and employs only about 15 persons. To maintain this volume of business has required about 4000 dealers. One of the greatest assets of the company is the esteem in which it is held by booksellers and stationers and their customers. In recent years, with the presence of television and of cheap pocket edition books, there has been a decline in bookplate sales. This has been compensated for by the development of specialized products printed on and die-cut from plastics.

With two or three minor exceptions all the stock of the company is owned by employees. At present all borrowing of working capital is done from them and not from banks. All but one of the directors are employees, one being elected by the employees at large, regardless of stock ownership. The one outside director is professor of business administration at Antioch College. The company has a profit *and loss* sharing system. Employees get eighty per cent of their wages each week; the balance is paid at the end of the year if earnings permit. Then, after a basic five per cent dividend is paid, the balance is shared equally between employees and stock-holders. There were a few tough depression and post war years when without the sharing of losses the company could scarcely have survived and the employees probably would have lost their positions. On the other hand, in good years shared profits have been a substantial addition to wages.

At one time the company made an effort to organize as a cooperative. However, the intense interest some of the members took in seeing that their associates maintained maximum production resulted in severe stresses among the less productive workers, and tempers sometimes wore thin. So by general agreement the plan was given up and a more conventional corporate form was adopted. Under this, however, the cooperative features have been developed successfully.

Recently the company had one of its periodic wage determinations. A committee elected by the employees, which incidentally included two members of the supervisory staff, went over the list of workers one by one, in each case proposing the wage for the ensuing year. This proposed wage list was then presented to the management, and was accepted without change. Ernest Morgan remarked on the thorough understanding of conditions and the moderateness and considerateness with which the proposals were made.

Wilda Pettiford, long time Bookplate Staff member, operating an automatic wrapping machine which applies cellophane to bookplate boxes.

Photo by H. Lee Jones

The Antioch Bookplate Company always has been as much a social and an economic adventure as a profit undertaking. A considerable part of the employees have been persons who for some reason needed a friendly lift. It was the first Yellow Springs industry to employ whites and Negroes without discrimination, though the practice is now general in the village. The company has employed Jewish refugees from Europe, Japanese from war relocation centers, and young men who had served prison sentences as conscientious objectors.

The strength of the firm is largely in the feeling of fellowship and solidarity which exists. More than once when a worker has been trained to a high degree of skill he has left for a war production or other job where he could get higher pay, and then has returned saying he had found that wages are not the only consideration in holding a job. The right to sick leave is so carefully respected by the workers that it almost never is used improperly. More frequently management finds it necessary to insist on its use. The range between high and low income in the company is considerably less than is usual in comparable businesses, and the social status of workers has little relation to relative income.

East meets West in the Bookplate Company Accounting Department. Jerry Noda, a Japanese-American, was evacuated from the west coast, and Marie Treuer escaped from Vienna. Mrs. Treuer subsequently became Assistant Treasurer of Vernay Laboratories.

A policy of sharing losses as well as profits usually is looked upon in industry as unworkable. It can succeed only where the spirit goes beyond what is called "good morale" and becomes mutual confidence, considerateness, and essential solidarity. Implicit in loss-sharing is the privilege of participating in the decisions through which profits and losses are made. The general participation by the workers in the affairs of the business gives an experience of sharing, and makes associates rather than "hired help". Also it discloses resources of information and sound judgment which only such participation would reveal.

2. The Antioch Press

The Antioch Press is the oldest of the modern Yellow Springs industries. Shortly after the reorganization of Antioch in 1921 it became evident that the college needed printing facilities not available locally. When occasion offered not long afterward, Dean Philip C. Nash purchased for the college the local newspaper and its printing plant. The paper was later given back to its former owner as not profitable for the college to publish. The printing plant was kept for college printing and for such job printing as was requested.

In 1923 it was decided to publish a college bulletin for publicity purposes. There being already hundreds of such, the problem of getting attention for the publication of a very small, unknown, midwestern college was formidable. An effort was made to produce a little magazine that would be in a class by itself, and not in competition with any other publication. This required distinction both in content and in appearance. No printing plant was found in Dayton or Springfield which provided the quality needed. A few issues were printed in New York, but it was difficult at such long range to maintain exacting quality control.

Under these circumstances it was decided to do the job ourselves in our own shop. Bruce Rogers, one of the foremost of American printers, advised on the layout of "Antioch Notes", selected a type face, advised on the quality of paper to use, and drew a design for a colophon or first page masthead. With this assistance the Antioch Press settled down to produce the quality of printing we wanted, and after a few issues, succeeded.

With college printing as a background, the Antioch Press has gradually extended its range. It now prints the *Antioch Review, Kenyon Review, Negro Educational Review, Journal of Physical Education, Individual Psychology Bulletin, Child Development, The Humanist, Antioch Alumni Bulletin,* and *Community Service News.* From time to time it publishes books. The Antioch Press has eleven employees. In give-and-take discussions in periodicals printed at the Press we have seen footnotes in which the linotype operator expressed his views on the subject being discussed. The fact that these were not eliminated by the author in proof reading indicated that they were apropos and were not considered as lese majesty. Is not life more interesting if those who do the manual work may now and then share in the adventure?

3. The Yellow Springs News

During the first forty or fifty years of its life, Yellow Springs intermittently supported a newspaper. Publication has been continuous since 1880. The trading area of Yellow Springs is very limited, extending only three or four miles beyond the village, so a local paper has a very limited field geographically. With practically every family taking the paper and nearly every merchant advertising, it is still a nip-and-tuck job to keep solvent. Nevertheless, the *News* is a very live eight-page weekly. Nearly all the reading matter originates in Yellow Springs, except for weekly letters from Congressmen. The *News* is sometimes controversial in a decent sort of way, and extremely independent in the views expressed. It has repeatedly received recognition for excellence in rural journalism. It would be very much of a letdown for the people of the village to have to depend on the usual small-town quality of newspaper. Probably not 20% of the readers agree with all the social and political views of the paper, but its columns are open to all shades of opinion, and they are quite commonly used.

The publisher of the *News* gave up a much more profitable and more secure place in the publishing field in order to have freedom to live and to work according to his convictions. He and his little staff have undergone and have survived an amount of hardship and opposition which very few would-be small town newspaper men will actually face.

Chapter VIII

THE FINE ARTS IN INDUSTRY

1. The Mazzolini Art Bronze Foundry

In the early days of the new Antioch, while I was searching for possible small industries to be associated with the college, a sculptor acquaintance told me about the "lost wax process" by which art bronzes are cast. This ancient art, descended from remote times in China and elsewhere, had not changed appreciably since it was described by Cellini about four hundred years ago. Since the art had survived so long in practice as the best way to make a true copy in bronze from an artist's model, it must have practical value. Not having been an object of modern research, without doubt it had undeveloped potentialities. Why should we not explore them?

The sculptor told me of a man who was teaching the lost wax process in his home country--Italy--who would like to come to America. After much red tape he finally arrived as an instructor at Antioch. An old, unused barn was acquired to work in, and word was passed around among Antioch students that we should like volunteers for a research project. Two upperclass students were interested, and began working. We located another Italian, Amos Mazzolini, in Dayton, who, while he had never seen the lost wax process, knew something of the ordinary sand casting of American brass foundries.

The work did not start off well. The two students, after perhaps a year, decided they were in a blind alley, with small prospect for success, and quit. Another who took their place did likewise. The man from Italy had simply used the Antioch opportunity to circumvent the immigration laws and shortly left for New York to work in the largest lost wax foundry in America.

When three students had quit we looked more carefully into the interests and qualifications of someone to replace them, and settled on a farmer boy from North Dakota. In his part-time work as an Antioch student he had done very well in a General Motors factory. We tried to picture to him the difficulties and uncertainties of the undertaking. After thinking it over he decided that he was interested. So this student, Morris Bean, joined Amos Mazzolini and they worked together.

Success did not come quickly. Little jobs and then larger ones were secured, but "red ink" persisted in the financial balance. We would gather a little money here and there to enable them to keep going. Morris Bean was graduated from the college and was married.

During this period the little foundry made some large castings. Among these are the bronze bases of the large flagpoles on the south side of the Archives building in Washington, D.C. These are some of the larger castings in the nation's capital. As a result of contacts made on that job Morris Bean began to experiment with aluminum.

The two men worked differently. Morris Bean was the laboratory scientist and practical administrator combined. Amos Mazzolini was artist and craftsman. As the work proceeded it became apparent that they were really traveling different roads, and the conclusion was reached that they should work independently of each other. Amos continued with bronze casting by the lost wax process, while Morris pursued his research in aluminum casting. From here on the aluminum foundry is a different story.

During the depression when art bronze casting was almost nonexistent, and later during the war when bronze was unobtainable, Mazzolini transformed his foundry building into an apartment house. (Morris Bean had retained the dairy barn while Amos Mazzolini had built another foundry which if necessary could be turned into residence quarters.) For a few years he did contracting and building for a living, and also taught modeling at Antioch. In whatever he worked at he did well, in the spirit of an intelligent master craftsman. When material became available again he built a new foundry, in which he has operated for several years.

Commissions for art bronze castings come to Mr. Mazzolini without solicitation from all over America as fast as he and his two or three assistants can handle them. He does not seek a large volume of business, but hopes to find and train one or two successors who can maintain his standards, and then he looks forward to less pressure of work and more leisure. He is artist as well as founder. Recently he completed a commission for a heroic size bust of Paderewski. He has also created designs for Heisey glass. He has taken time to build a commodious and pleasant home at the edge of the village with a large, light basement for his workshop. His college class in modeling continues to be a live interest.

2. The Metcalf Stained Glass Studios

Stained glass is nothing new to Robert Metcalf. When he left art school in Philadelphia in 1925 he went to work for a concern in that field in Reading, Pennsylvania, where he remained for three years. Then, after a month or two with John Gordon Guthrie in New York, he joined the Henry Wynd Young stained glass studio, also in New York, where he was in charge for two years. When the studio burned in 1930 he started his own at Closter, near Englewood, New Jersey. From 1934 until 1942 he was with the Dayton Art Institute, and then in visual education at Wright Field (aeronautical research). Since 1945 he has been at Yellow Springs where he has combined teaching art at the college and operating his stained glass studio.

Metcalf's commissions come from many localities, although most of them are from New York City, Washington, Dayton and Cleveland. He has five employees, some of whom he trained at Antioch.

MRS. METCALF AT WORK IN METCALF STAINED GLASS STUDIO

Mr. Metcalf is strongly of the opinion that being outside New York and in a midwest village is no handicap. He says that people who objected to crossing the George Washington Bridge to visit his studio in New Jersey now do not seem to hesitate to take a plane for Yellow Springs. The village, he holds, is a much better place to work than the city. There is less pressure and crowding. One may miss day-by-day contact with current work in his field, but Metcalf does not want that. "People with a job to do are inclined to spend too much time looking at what other people do." The metropolis is confusing, and the artist tends to lose perspective. Much of the creative art of Europe, he holds, was done in small communities. He hopes to see a group in his field in Yellow Springs, but that it will not be too big a group, and that the same will be true in other art fields.

3. The Vie Design Company

In 1946 Read Viemeister was a twenty-four-year-old product designer in New York, working on a salary as director of styling for J. Gordon Lippincott, industrial designers. Being engaged to a New York girl, Beverly Lipsett, who was then an Antioch student, he came out to see her. Both of them felt that they were "fed up" with the city. Result--he decided to cut loose, and came to live in Yellow Springs. He married Beverly without waiting for her to graduate. Now they have three children--children being a Yellow Springs habit.

Having made the rash leap, Viemeister found himself without work. What could a design artist do in Yellow Springs? He got a designing job now and then in the neighboring cities, Columbus, Dayton, Cincinnati, all within 65 miles. The nows and thens gradually became more frequent until he found himself head of a business in industrial design. He took in a partner, Budd Steinhilber, 26 years old, and another Yellow Springs small industry was off to a good start.

VIE DESIGN STUDIO

All is grist that comes to the Vie Design mill. Power lawnmowers are uninteresting things. A manufacturer wished his could be beautiful as well as efficient. Vie Design tackled the job. The same with bicycles and electric fans. A wire recorder needs an attractive exterior. Chevrolet and Buick steering wheels need their faces lifted. Furniture makers want modern designs. And so on.

What about Yellow Springs as the site for such an urbanized, specialized business? Viemeister says clients like to come to his attractive modern studio at the edge of the village. There is no comparison in convenience of living. Many hours are saved from commuting. The only disadvantage he found is that there is as yet no photostat machine in Yellow Springs.

4. Major Delano P. Foote: Industrial Design

During the past three years Major Foote has developed a practice in textile design for printed fabrics, and in wallpaper design. In addition he works in the fine arts doing painting and lithography. His clients are mostly in Ohio and New York. To enter this field Major Foote stepped quite aside from his previous many years of experience, and has broken or ignored some of the axioms of conventional business. Most industrial designers, and most sales of industrial designs, are in New York. Yet after having grown up in Brooklyn and having worked about 20 years in building materials and in air conditioning he chose Yellow Springs as the locus for his work.

Major Foote was in the First World War for two years, and then reverted to inactive status in the reserves. During the Second World War he was in the Air Force in the European and Mediterranean Theaters on staff and liaison duty. While at Wright and Patterson Air Fields preparing for field service, he and Mrs. Foote lived in nearby Yellow Springs. He relates that during his field service when he thought of home he thought not of Brooklyn and Manhattan, where he had spent most of his civilian life, but of Yellow Springs.

When, at the close of the Second World War, he returned to Wright-Patterson Fields for transfer to inactive status in the reserves, he determined to burn the bridges to his past industrial activities and to seek a career in art. For years his interest had been in this direction, but business responsibilities precluded study in that field. At the age of 53 he enrolled in a four year course in fine and applied arts at the Dayton Art Institute. During this period he also studied painting in the summer at the Fine Art Center in Colorado Springs, Colorado. On completing the Art Institute course in 1950 he set up a studio in a barn and undertook to develop a practice in industrial art design.

Major Foote has been surprisingly productive during the three years he has maintained his studio. His designs for cloth prints, drapes, and wallpapers, have quickly won a market. Demand for his paintings is more and more competing with that for his industrial art.

Part of his satisfaction is because he and Mrs. Foote find the village of Yellow Springs a pleasant and stimulating environment. He particularly enjoys the primeval forest of "Glen Helen" with its brooks, its rock cliffs and its great trees. The Glen furnishes him many subjects for design.

To begin a four year training course in a new field at 53 and then, at the completion of that course to undertake to make a living at the new calling, suggests a quality of daring and of imagination that is rare. The fact that Yellow Springs is a village where such things are done makes it an interesting place to live, and tends to draw others of similar independent spirit.

5. Photographic Studios in Yellow Springs

A village of 2500, especially having a contributory trade area with a radius of only three or four miles, as is the case with Yellow Springs, would commonly be considered too small to support one photographer. Yet Yellow Springs has three studios, and two or three other photographers maintain part-time businesses. They find the village to be a suitable location for their work.

It all started in the late 1920's when an upper-class student, H. Lee Jones, paid his way at college by operating a photographic studio of much more than ordinary quality. He employed two other students under the Antioch work-and-study program. When Jones graduated in 1926 he sold his studio to one of these students, who soon sold it to the other, Axel Bahnsen. Axel was from a Danish family that had lived for many years in France from where he came to Antioch.

Gradually the photographic world began to take notice of him. His work had favorable recognition in national exhibitions. His articles on the art and philosophy of photography were welcome in photographic magazines. He became active in the Photographic Society of America. His reputation spread by word of mouth until now people come from a radius of a hundred miles for his work. In addition he has a national mail order business in developing color films.

Bahnsen feels he should know something of the personality of his subject before taking a photograph. So an engagement begins with a friendly visit. Only when he thinks circumstances are favorable is he ready to take a picture.

Making a living by photography is not enough. Anything one does, he thinks, should be interesting in itself. Bahnsen was surprised to find that this interest was not a luxury which he indulged, but that it actually resulted in a desirable class of business.

He feels that photography must develop its own philosophy and code of ethics. One can misrepresent by photography as well as by words. As it becomes a major means of communication, unless it does develop adequate philosophy and ethics its great possibilities may miscarry. A picture should be truly representative.

Bahnsen holds that to an increasing extent the picture is displacing the written word, and it will continue to do so. Consider modern periodicals--*Life*, *Time*, the *Saturday Evening Post*. The written word and photography, along with radio and television, are phases of a single process--communication. Colleges and universities should change their departments of journalism to departments of communication and should develop and present underlying principles for using all media. Bahnsen asks himself, how can photographers be educated to be representative. He is working at developing photography for magazine use and generally as a communication medium.

Bahnsen conducts a private seminar for photographers from Yellow Springs and surrounding cities. Asked about the competition created by his seminar, he replied that competition often is a state of mind; that the various photographers supplement each other, and that there is more business in the village than if there were only one photographer.

Eleanor Bahnsen, Axel's wife, has received international honors for her color photography, and has been a judge or exhibited her color slides in many national and international exhibits, receiving an award recently from Tokyo. She assists Axel in his work and makes most of the prints of his pictures.

Anton and Antoinette Schreiber have their well-equipped studio for child portraiture, where the effort is to capture the true character of children and childhood. This requires not only a sound knowledge of photography, but of childhood as well. They had a reputation in this field before leaving New York. While child photography would seem to be a specialty beyond the capacity of a village to support, their practice ranges far beyond its limits. With a comprehensive background in photographic engineering, Anton has done research in color, as well as in black and white, and his original work, recognized in technical literature, has resulted in a research contract with the U.S. Air Forces.

The third full-time studio is that of Mack Schwab. As a photographer of children he serves patrons who come from Dayton, Cincinnati and Springfield. His photos have been reproduced in *Woman's Day* and *Parents' Magazine*.

John Raney works as electronics engineer at the Wright-Patterson Air Force Base ten miles away. As a supplement to his regular work he does children's portraits. He has tried to retire from photography but has been unable to do so. He has a hobby, too, of nature photography. He was a member of Bahnsen's class. He thinks Yellow Springs an ideal place for a photographic center. He and his wife became interested in Yellow Springs and have bought a home there. He says he would not trade the town for any other in that part of the country. He can support a semi-hobby and find it accepted.

David Kirkpatrick, another photographer, is works manager of Rike's large department store in Dayton. He does work for exhibitions. He was one of about a dozen in Axel Bahnsen's seminar. He says that Axel is a stimulating teacher, gives himself freely, and has become a national figure in the field of photography.

In addition to these professional or semi-professional photographers the village also has a pure amateur who has a national reputation for his out-of-doors and his still-life pictures. This is Russell Stewart, president of the local Miami Deposit Bank. Thus there exists in the village a sort of photographic fraternity. With one possible exception, none of those concerned think of the small size of their community as being a handicap. The one possible exception is concerned with certain personal and social factors rather than with economic possibilities.

Chapter IX

IN THE SERVICE OF AGRICULTURE

1. Dewine and Hamma: Farm Seeds

In point of sales volume the largest industry in Yellow Springs is that of the Dewine and Hamma farm seed firm. Some Yellow Springs industries were the direct or the indirect outcome of activities of Antioch College, but others owed nothing to its presence unless, perhaps, the habit of starting such things was unconsciously contagious. The Dewine and Hamma firm never had any connection with the college, or any help from it.

About 1925 a small feed business which was operated on the main street in Yellow Springs failed and went out of business. The only employees of the proprietor had been two young men, George Dewine and H.D. Hamma. Dewine, being out of a job, started a little business for himself, buying eggs from the farmers, and selling them feed for cattle and hogs. A little later Hamma joined him. For several years they continued this business, also operating a hay baler.

At that time farm seed was sold at feed and seed stores, the farmer being required to come to the store for it and to haul it home. To plant a forty-acre field of wheat called for two or three tons of seed, and at that time many farmers did not have trucks for hauling. It occurred to Dewine and Hamma to deliver the seed. Dewine would canvass the neighboring farms and take orders, which would then be delivered by Hamma in a trailer hitched to his auto. They did not just sell seed, but studied the farmers' needs and how to supply them. After a few years they discontinued other lines and gave nearly their whole attention to seeds. In about 1935 they purchased the defunct corn canning plant on a railroad siding at the edge of the village, and moved their business there. In recent years a son, Dick Dewine, has become a member of the firm and carries the major load of research and development.

Neither the Dewines nor Hamma had any technical schooling for this work, but they deliberately went about trying to understand every phase of the farmers' needs as related to seed. Touch almost any element of their work and one gets intelligent, interesting answers. For instance, when I asked whether it is good practice to buy bluegrass seed gathered from the wild prairies of northern Minnesota, to be planted in Kentucky where the climate is very different, I was given an interesting and informed talk on planting seed far from its place of origin. In the case of bluegrass, I was told, seed raised in northern Minnesota, or on the relatively dry Nebraska prairies, did better in Kentucky than the native strains.

The farmer wants to purchase seed that does not bring weed pests into his fields. As I watched the varied and elaborate processes for removing every kind of seed but the kind to be planted, I could see why farmers all over the central and eastern states have come to rely on this source

DEWINE & HAMMA PLANT. SEED BEING PROPERLY MIXED, BULKED AND PACKED.

of supply. Seed was passed over velvet rollers which held
back that with a rough coat; it was joggled across a sloping
surface at just such a rate that too heavy seeds would be
discarded on one side and too light ones on the other, thus
leaving seed to be saved to fall into its proper channel.
Seed was mixed with slightly moist sawdust and joggled across
another surface; certain seed stuck to the sawdust. Light
seed and chaff were blown out by an air blast. Another cleaning device took out all but that of a certain length. Elsewhere seed was separated according to its shape. It is rare
weed seed that escapes all these cleaning processes. Red top
seed loses as much as a quarter of its weight in being
cleaned; timothy seed about six per cent. The waste is ground
and sold for hog feed.

One of their principal lines is seed wheat. This is grown
near by under their direct supervision. Each wheat field is
carefully gone over by trained men who pull out weeds, "off

varieties" and unhealthy plants. In processing it, light seed is blown out by air, and the seed passes through eight different screens to get rid of weeds and shriveled grains. It is tested for weight, moisture, disease, purity and germination. Each grain is coated with a chemical disinfectant which not only frees the seed from disease but sterilizes the surrounding soil so that the seed has a good chance to grow. As a result of this care, according to the firm, they grow and process more Ohio certified wheat seed than any other company in the state. Seed wheat treated in this way may bear 25, or 30% more than that which is not treated.

Sometimes new developments bring about striking changes. About ten years ago a patch of grass was noted on a Kentucky hillside which during a dry season remained green and good for pasture. According to Dick Dewine it seems to be identical with a variety native to the Pacific Northwest, and may have been introduced by accident. Experiment station specialists have spread knowledge of it and now, only ten years later, this grass, "Kentucky fescue," is planted to the extent of more than half a million acres a year. Such an expansion of use calls for a source of seed. In the rough, hilly parts of southeastern Ohio there was much poor land which was being abandoned for agriculture, and which could be bought for $15 to $25 an acre. This proves to be good for raising Kentucky fescue seed, and now many of these farms are producing the seed in crops that are worth $100 an acre a year. Practically all of this Ohio crop is purchased and distributed by Dewine and Hamma.

The timothy seed market has had an interesting revolution. Formerly Ohio imported its supply, but with the introduction of the combine harvester it can be harvested practicably in the state. Dewine and Hamma, alert to new possibilities, soon led Ohio in marketing timothy seed, and in 1951 were the country's largest dealers in it.

Of the between fifty and a hundred varieties of farm seed in which they deal they treat many varieties chemically. With some glossy-coated seed the chemical tends to fall off before the seed is planted. When I visited the plant I found them experimenting with coating the seed with an adhesive which would make the disinfectant stick to it, but would not make the seeds stick together. Such constant exploring is one price they have paid for their success.

Much of the best seed of some varieties comes from the Pacific or Mountain states or from the Great Plains. Whether their purchases are made from the Pacific Coast states or nearer by, practically all are made by telephone. The purchases are mostly received by carload for processing, the company having storage space for sixty-five carloads. Delivery within one hundred and fifty miles is made by a fleet of trucks, beyond that by railroad in carload lots. The sales area is from the Mississippi to the New England states and to the Southeast. Sales, like purchases, are mostly made by telephone. In 1951 they amounted to $2,500,000, and their business is steadily growing. The firm has about 30 employees.

What might have remained just a small country town business of buying and selling seed has become an intelligent process of raising, selecting, buying, cleaning, sterilizing, drying, packing, marketing and shipping. Just good, steady, persistent, intelligent work has made the difference.

DEWINE & HAMMA SUPERVISE THE GROWING OF THEIR SEED WHEAT

2. The Grinnell Farm Equipment Company

Cornelius Grinnell still lives on the old family place where more than a century ago his grandfather built a home and bought the sturdy waterpower grist mill, which still stands. Cornelius believed in adequate power equipment for farming, but his father's relatively small farm did not justify the necessary expense. So he bought good equipment and when it was not needed on the home farm he made it pay by doing machine work on neighboring farms by contract.

Then on one occasion he went to Indiana to buy a farm elevator from a manufacturer who had no sales organization in Ohio. Cornelius persuaded the manufacturer to give him an agency for selling the elevator on a retail basis. The manufacturer was pleased with the sales he made, and appointed Grinnell as wholesale agent for Ohio. With a good record in selling this piece of equipment, Grinnell secured similar wholesale agencies from other firms, until he now has thirty such accounts. At first he sold both wholesale and retail, but now he sells at wholesale only. As the business has increased he has employed salesmen, and now needs three to cover the retail dealers of the state.

By a natural course of events Grinnell has become one of those links in the business chain which enables small industries to secure distribution of their products without the necessity of maintaining widespread sales organizations for each firm. More than half the lines he carries are made in Iowa, usually by small town small industries. On one trip to Iowa looking for lines to represent he made connections with ten such firms. Considering all the lines of small industry in our country and the many states or regions to be served, there probably is room for scores of such distributing organizations. In the few years Grinnell has been engaged in this business his sales have reached about $500,000 a year.

Chapter X

MISCELLANEOUS ECONOMIC ACTIVITIES

1. Paul Dawson: *Brick Supply*

Such an account as this should have at least one Horatio Alger story. Mr. Dawson was born in Yellow Springs in 1901, as one of 12 children. His schooling stopped with the first year of high school, though he read nearly every book in the local library. From the age of 14 to 19 he worked on a nearby farm. Until he was 12 years old he never got as far from home as Springfield, 10 miles distant, though a trolley line ran between the towns.

At 19 he tried to get a local railroad job, but was told he was too small. He went to Columbus, where he tried for a railroad job with no better results, and then on to Pittsburgh, where he did get a job, and spent 7 years as a railroad switchman and brakeman. Improvements in railroad methods kept reducing the number of railway employees needed. With low seniority he had repeated temporary layoffs, during which he held about 25 temporary jobs. He saw his fellow railroad men growing old on their jobs, waiting for retirement and pensions, fearful lest some accident or mistake might lead to dismissal and loss of security, and he decided to try something else. In two years spent in a Columbus, Ohio, machine shop he saw the other workmen in a sort of treadmill, and he began to wish he could be "on his own."

A brother-in-law in North Carolina was working for a company that was pioneering in distribution of propane gas-- the "bottled gas" used in rural homes. He got a distributing job with the company, and for three and a half years travelled over the adjoining parts of North Carolina, Virginia and Tennessee getting dealers. Then in 1931 he took over some Florida territory for the same company. The depression caught the firm much overextended, and in an effort to keep solvent it steadily cut down the compensation of its sales representatives, until Dawson's income was too small to live on, and he had used up his savings. Late in 1932, with $200 left, he bought an old Chevrolet car for $100 and started north with his wife, reaching Yellow Springs about Christmas with $20 in cash. After nearly 18 years as a working man he was back to where he had started, and financially not much better off.

For a time he and his wife lived with his parents. In 1931, while the depression was near its worst, my son and a few friends and I started the "Yellow Springs Exchange," where people could bring anything they could spare or produce and exchange it for what they needed. Dawson's mother made cakes which she turned in for what the family wanted most.

No jobs were to be had, except on relief. Paul Dawson persuaded the local Chevrolet dealer to sell him a rattle-trap truck chassis for $100, and in payment to take his 90 day note with interest at 8%. A local automobile dealer refused him credit of $15 to buy gas. He had enough to get to Dayton, 20 miles away, where he bought from a junk yard an old truck body for $17. That left him cash assets of $3.00. He bought 5 gallons of gas, and drove home to put his truck in order.

He had no auto license. He asked a nearby flour miller for a loan of $30, to be repaid by hauling wheat, and was refused. However, he kept pressing the miller for a loan, and finally got it. The license cost $29.75. He hauled wheat for this miller, and sand and gravel wherever he could get orders. When he began to get on his feet he and his wife left his father's home and rented rooms over an old store building. He began to haul coal from the mines in eastern Ohio, to sell wherever he could find customers. In developing a coal and gravel business he needed a telephone for receiving orders, and he and his wife discussed whether they could afford the $2.00 a month investment.

A contractor repairing an Antioch building employed him to haul brick from Cincinnati, 65 miles away, and this gave him an idea. The brick had already been shipped by railroad from the brick making plant to Cincinnati. Why not haul direct from the brick kiln to the job. He went to each of the 8 brick dealers in Dayton and tried to arrange to haul brick for them, but not one of them would use his services.

While hauling coal Dawson frequently had passed a large brickmaking plant at McArthur, Ohio. He visited the 70-year-old proprietor, found he had no dealer in Dayton (the former dealer, caught in the depression, had committed suicide), and arranged to buy brick to sell there. The roads of Ohio were just getting into condition to make truck hauling practicable. Dawson searched around Dayton until he got an order for 10,000 brick, and with that first sale a new kind of business was begun. Up to that time all Ohio brick not used in the immediate vicinity of where it was made was shipped by railroad. The method started by Mr. Dawson has increased until now 60% or 80% of that used in the state is shipped by truck.

Mr. Dawson bought his first new truck in January, 1934, arranging for the smallest possible down payment and as long payment period as possible. He bought his second new truck in April of the same year. At first a sale and delivery of 15,000 brick a week seemed good; now sales run about 150,000 a week. His annual sales are $200,000 to $300,000 a year, of which between 5% and 10% is net profit.

The business is carried on with a very small staff. He has three truck drivers. His larger trucks carry 6000 brick at a load, worth about $300. Dawson circulates around southwestern Ohio making contact with prospective purchasers. His wife answers the telephone when he is out, and a part time accountant comes in periodically to keep his books and to make out tax reports. A room in his attractive home serves as office and sample room. On one day recently 23 prospects called in person, and most of them made purchases. At first he had a single source of supply; now he buys from 8 brick companies.

Dawson has set limits to his operations. He sells only where a round trip can be made by truck in one day--about 150 miles from where the brick are made to where they are used. On his selling trips he seldom gets so far away that he cannot spend the night at home. He has made favorable real estate investments, has developed two real estate subdivisions adjoining the village, and is one of the larger local property owners.

It may seem that his business was based on accidental good fortune. However, favorable "accidents" tend to happen to active and observant people. He remarks, "There is seldom a circumstance but that there is some way to handle it." Paul Dawson's business, like that of Cornelius Grinnell, is interesting in that it has resulted in, or has coincided with, a fundamental change in a distribution process. It was by taking advantage of economies made possible by the new technology that he succeeded. He thinks it would be harder to start today than even 17 years ago when he began, largely because of the swarm of tax and other examiners who come to look into the business, and because of the numerous government reports required. Some of them find it hard to believe that he carries on a business of such size with no inventory.

2. W.B. Dawson: Earth Moving Equipment

William Dawson, a brother of Paul, was a clerk in a local grocery store. Wanting to work for himself, he acquired a truck and began hauling sand and gravel. Then he would drive to a coal mine in eastern Ohio, buy a load of coal and sell it in the west part of the state. This helped during the depression period. As the years passed he has acquired a good gravel deposit and sells gravel for various purposes. To this he has added bulldozers, excavating equipment and land clearing machinery. Altogether he has come to be the principal local source of supply for gravel and sand, and the chief local reliance over a considerable area for land clearing, the making of farm ponds, and for similar construction work.

3. The Odiorne Industrial Advertising Agency: Louise Odiorne, Landscape Architect

Sometimes one calling is not enough for a family. Louise Harris, granddaughter of Wallace Carr who pioneered in the propagation of evergreens by cuttings and was proprietor of the old Yellow Springs Nursery, attended Antioch for two and a half years before transferring to Ohio State University, where she was graduated, prepared for a career in landscape architecture. Then she married Dick Odiorne, a graduate of Massachusetts Institute of Technology, and began to raise a family. They decided they wanted to live in Yellow Springs. For a time Richard Odiorne commuted to nearby cities to work, and then followed the Yellow Springs habit of starting his own business. The result is the Odiorne Industrial Advertising Agency, established in 1948.

The firm is not in competition with standard advertising agencies. Working chiefly for manufacturers of technical products, it prepares technical literature, text and illustrations, publicity articles and advertisements. It works for such firms as Robbins and Myers, manufacturers of electrical equipment, the Flamatic Division of the Cincinnati Milling Machine Company, and the Aircraft Automotive Division of the Surface Combustion Corporation. The firm has four employees, and its own studio.

Meanwhile Louise Odiorne continues her work in landscape architecture, getting as far away as Florida on her jobs, to the extent that her young family will permit. They built a combined studio and home, so that the overhead is low, even if the children are under foot.

Louise Odiorne has as her chief interest the planning of the immediate environment of the home. She is interested not only in the appearance of the home setting from outside, but the intimate nearby prospects from inside. Each window in the house is a point of view from which the nearby landscaping is done.

4. The Carr Evergreen Nursery

While most Yellow Springs industries and related activities had their birth in modern technology, one of the smallest is a survival from an earlier age, though in its day it, too, was a pioneer.

In 1869 Wallace Carr established a nursery at the edge of the village. Being of an experimental turn he tried to prop-

COLD FRAMES FOR ROOTING EVERGREEN CUTTINGS AT CARR NURSERIES

agate evergreens from cuttings, and succeeded in doing so. As he was a pioneer in this field, his business expanded until it reached from coast to coast, most sales being in wholesale lots to other nurserymen. On his death in 1933 his son, Ed Carr, continued the business.

Knowledge of the technique for rooting evergreen cuttings has become widespread, and there is now no element of monopoly in the business. It continues on an even keel, as it has for 83 years, but with only five employees, and with annual sales of about $20,000. The nursery is an attractive spot in the village. Mr. Carr says that the size of the town does not make much difference in his business. He is a member of the National Association of Nurserymen, which helps him to a wide acquaintance.

5. Loes' Kennels

The Leroy Loes have a farm on the margin of Yellow Springs. Some years ago, as a hobby, Mrs. Loe began raising cocker spaniel pups for sale. The hobby developed into a full-time business, and the market now covers a considerable part of the country. The Loes have rented their farm, keeping a small tract on which they have built a comfortable home, and both are engaged in the new business.

Several other economic or social activities have been developed which are somewhat unusual for a village of 2500 people. Among these are a well equipped medical clinic with five physicians and a staff of technicians and assistants; a little movie theater which shows more of the world's great pictures than other Ohio cities that are 25 times as large; a well housed and directed village library; a credit union, two active building contractor firms, a heating contractor, and a practising architect.

Chapter XI

INDUSTRIES WHICH MOVED AWAY, FAILED,
OR DISCONTINUED

Of the little industries which started at Yellow Springs, some moved to other locations, while others failed or for other reasons were discontinued. A mention of them is necessary in order to give a representative picture of the degree of success of such undertakings.

Industries Which Moved Away

1. DRIERITE. Mr. W.A. Hammond was a member of the chemistry faculty at Antioch. About 1930 he began to talk to some of his associates about what seemed to him to be an industrial possibility. He said the ceramics industry of the state had a large amount of waste material to dispose of. Some of this is very hygroscopic, that is, it has a strong tendency to absorb water. The material, he said, is easily purified, and then would be valuable as a drying agent, to remove water where it is not wanted.

In the laboratory he worked out methods of purification and packaging and use. Then he rented a small space in the village and employed one or two people to process the material and prepare it for sale. The market for his product, called "drierite," grew rapidly, and soon he rented larger working space, resigned from his college position, and was in business for himself. Manufacturers of refrigerators put drierite between the outside and inside walls of the refrigerator to insure dry insulation. As telephone cables are spliced a little drierite is put where it will absorb any chance moisture which might affect insulation. Also, it became standard laboratory material over the country.

As business increased he moved again, this time into the largest available space in the village. Then came the war, and new industrial building was not allowed unless given priority. Still the demand increased. Hammond found an available industrial building in Xenia, ten miles away, where he has since been located. In terms of net profits we understand this business is one of the two or three most successful of those that have developed at Yellow Springs.

2. HYBRID CORN. In the late 1920's, before the "New Deal"
came into existence, Henry Wallace was developing and producing hybrid seed corn in Iowa. An Antioch biology student had
a "co-op" job with the company, and after graduation became
manager of Wallace's central office. He interested the Antioch
biology faculty in the research. Then an arrangement was made
whereby Antioch would cooperate with the firm--the Pioneer
Hybrid Corn Co.--in raising and processing the seed. As the
project grew through the years a processing plant was built
on the Antioch campus, and sales of seed reached $500,000 a
year. They were made over most of Ohio and Pennsylvania.

There were a number of reasons for the project's leaving
Yellow Springs. During the late 1930's and the early 40's
the administration of Antioch was not enthusiastic over college association in business, and disposed of all operating
interests except the Antioch Press, which was directly needed for college work, and the Hybrid Corn Company withdrew
its operations from Yellow Springs. Aside from a local branch
lumber yard this was the only "branch industry" experience
in recent Yellow Springs history.

3. ANTIOCH SHOES. When the new Antioch program was initiated in 1921, one of the very definite elements of the
program, as part of a well-proportioned education, was concern for student health. In my conversations with the college
physician he repeatedly mentioned health difficulties of girl
students which he imputed to improper posture resulting from
the general wearing of high-heeled shoes. To get a more
accurate judgment in the matter I took occasion to question
a number of representative orthopedists. In brief, they said
that high-heeled shoes were the basis of a considerable part
of their practice. The posture compelled by such shoes, they
said, set up strains and brought about misplacements which
might be more serious than the public realized.

With that general opinion I began to search for a source
of footwear which would be acceptable. To my surprise I
found that very little work had been done by the shoe industry on the anatomy and physiology of the human foot with a
view to the proper design of shoes.

While this search was going on I met a remarkable character, Edward Mathews. His business was that of designing shoe
machinery, but his chief interest, his controlling passion,

was the design and manufacture of shoes that would give freedom to the foot. No missionary to the heathen ever worked with more zeal to save souls than did Mathews to save feet. He had developed a last and a design for women's shoes, the product of years of experiment which, he assured me, could be put into production on a modest scale with an investment of only about $4000. I brought him to Antioch to help us work out our idea.

We soon decided that we had better not undertake shoe manufacture for the present. We would design the shoes, superintend their manufacture, and carry through their promotion and sale. First we worked with the Clapp Shoe Company of Massachusetts, a small, old firm, with the highest standards of integrity and with fine workmanship. They were so impressed with Mathews' insight and ability that they financed the undertaking for a few years. Their limitation was that, as makers of men's shoes they found difficulty in giving their shoes the lightness and airiness of style which women's shoes called for.

As Mathews went about the country he constantly visited shoe factories and talked with shoe designers. He sensitized much of the shoe industry to the need for considering the anatomy of the human foot in designing shoes, and in my opinion had more to do with the emergence of rational shoe design than perhaps any other person in the country. He secured many excellent retail outlets for Antioch Shoes, and they began to be quite well known.

Although Mathews was a person of great insight, with exceptional artistic sense and tremendous drive, he lacked balance. In his enthusiasm he would promise more than he could deliver. He constantly leaped ahead to new undertakings before being well grounded in what already was under way. He would disregard budgets. After several years of trying to work with this brilliant and creative, but ungovernable personality, we parted company with him and turned the shoe project over to Mr. Lloyd Snook. Thereupon it continued, less brilliantly and creatively but more stably. Under Mr. Snook the project paid its way, but only slowly developed toward a substantial earning position.

At the close of the Second World War, in line with the general policy of disposing of its industrial interests, the college turned over the project to Mr. Snook. Much of the

work already was being done at the factory where the shoes
were actually built, the Selby Shoe Company of Portsmouth,
Ohio, and with the disposal of the project the last tie with
Yellow Springs was severed. The business still continues.

Each of the three businesses mentioned as having left
Yellow Springs continues to operate successfully. Each one,
with the possible exception of Hybrid Corn, continues under
the same management as it had in our village.

Industries Which Failed or Discontinued

In the starting of numerous business ventures it is usual
that some failures should be mixed with the successes. The
Yellow Springs experience is no exception, though the proportion of failures and discontinuences is not large.

1. LANDSCAPING. During the 1920's two Antioch students
undertook to pay their way through college by raising nursery
stock and landscaping small homes where the services of a
professional landscape architect never would be called for.
They furnished the plants, provided the layout, and did the
planting. They raised shrubs commonly in demand, purchasing
the remainder. The little business was reasonably successful
until the leader, Stanley Brewster, becoming more interested
in landscaping as a profession, transferred to a university
which gave courses and a degree in landscape architecture,
where he graduated. He has since come to have considerable
recognition in that field. With his leaving the project was
discontinued.

2. CABINET MAKING. In the late 1920's an Antioch student,
unusually proficient in fine carpentry and cabinet making,
desired to start a cabinet making business. With a faculty
member as counsellor and associate he began working in a
rented building near the village. After a period of filling
miscellaneous small orders a prospect appeared which seemed
to offer opportunity for rapid expansion. A new York City firm
presented what for the little shop was a very large order.
At very considerable effort and investment, material was as-
sembled and the order was filled and shipped to New York.
Inquiry concerning the responsibility of the New York firm
had been inadequate. It went through the process of bankruptcy,
and thus evaded paying for the order. This circumstance was
a shock to the student cabinet maker. During his work he had
become aware that satisfactory work would call for a plant

with humidity and temperature control, and he did not want
to commit himself to the long time effort involved. So the
project was discontinued.

3. THE GOLDEN DOOR MAGAZINE. During the depression o f
the 1930's an Antioch graduate undertook to publish a new
magazine, *The Golden Door*, of which each monthly issue was
to be a collection of short, little known literary master-
pieces. The format was similar to that of the *Reader's Digest*.
This young man had slender resources, but his expenses were
low, the little magazine seemed well received, and success
seemed a possibility. The firm which handled the distribution
of the magazine on newsstands became quite enthusiastic and
indicated that it could use a very much larger edition, to
be sold on consignment. It took all the capital the young
man could assemble to meet this sudden growth of demand, but
for a few issues the larger number were printed and delivered.
Then it turned out that the news distributing firm had made a
wildly optimistic guess, and most of the magazines were returned unsold. Sales were climbing fast enough so that with
small additional capital, even to the extent of $10,000 or
$15,000,the project probably could have weathered the shock.
However, the money was not available and the magazine was
discontinued. The striking success of this young man in
later undertakings suggests that with a more fortunate turn
of circumstance, or with better informed counsel, he might
have succeeded.

4. THE OSTER HATCHERY. During the 1920's Ralph Oster
developed a considerable business in selling day old chicks,
hatched in a modern plant. The business continued profitably
for about 15 years, then, Mr. Oster wishing to retire from
active work, the business was discontinued. There was no
element of business failure.

This, then, is the list of businesses which did not succeed or which were discontinued. Possibly a few other frail
one-man efforts were begun and discontinued during this period.
The major part of the little industrial efforts succeeded and
have continued.

YELLOW SPRINGS BROOK IN GLEN HELEN

Chapter XII

HOW YELLOW SPRINGS SMALL INDUSTRIES BEGAN TO FIND THEIR MARKETS

A score of undertakings in Yellow Springs do not begin to illustrate all the methods that might be used to find a market. They do illustrate the truth that in nearly every case there is at least one feasible and natural way to proceed, and that the problem is to find and use such methods rather than arbitrarily to follow any conventional rules about selling. An account of some of the methods used by the village industries may be suggestive.

Often opportunity comes seemingly by accident. Probably most people meet with accidental circumstances which if recognized and taken full advantage of might be the bases for successful careers. That was the way with the Antioch Foundry (later named Morris Bean and Company).

While Amos Mazzolini and Morris Bean were making bronze castings, in filling one contract they used a worker skilled in plaster molds. This man was later employed by the Goodyear Rubber Company, and while there mentioned to his superiors the high quality of work he had seen in the Antioch Foundry. The Goodyear Company was not satisfied with the quality of their tire molds, and asked the Antioch Foundry whether they could do such work. Mazzolini and Bean knew nothing about aluminum casting, and the desired work had little if anything in common with the processes used by the foundry. A natural course would have been to give that answer to the inquiry, and to drop the subject. However, Morris Bean proposed a program of research to be financed by the Goodyear Company. The proposal was accepted, and after 8 months of research there emerged an entirely new method, now known to the trade as the Antioch Process, which has been the basis for the success of the Foundry. From there on it was largely a matter of doing a first rate job for one customer and letting the quality of the work sell itself to others. Naturally, a constant program of research and experiment was necessary to reduce costs, improve quality, and keep the process in line with the times and adapted to new applications.

The Yellow Springs Instrument Company got its foothold by making laboratory equipment for Antioch College and for the

Fels Research Institute associated with the college. Then Mr. Hooven, industrial consultant and Antioch faculty member, had a client who needed certain laboratory equipment, and turned the job over to the young men who constituted the new company. He also introduced them at the U.S. aircraft laboratories at Wright Field, where there was need for special laboratory equipment. As visitors to the Fels Institute saw equipment which the young firm had made they told their own institutions about it. Also, the salesmen who came to sell material or tools to the new company would tell them of need for new equipment which they had observed elsewhere, and made contacts which resulted in orders.

Bollinger says the business has just grown, they scarcely know how. With increased facilities for production they are beginning to need more business, and are circulating a brochure describing the company and its products. This is bringing a response and lively interest. Their most dependable outlet is an old and highly regarded firm which sells laboratory equipment.

The Nosker brothers got their start from the fact that their brother, working at the U.S. aircraft laboratories, found some research equipment to be inadequate. That was not unusual. Most of us find some of the things we use to be imperfect. The brothers took one unsatisfactory item and worked at it until it served its purpose. With that well done, a market was ready for them.

Velsey granite surface plates were suggested by accidental circumstance. However, the beginning of finding a market was a process of fairly orderly exploration. When Mr. Velsey had perfected his product he carefully prepared an advertising sheet telling about its qualities, and sent copies to firms having physical research problems. He received one reply for each 20 of the statements sent out, and to about half of this 5% he made sales. Also he called personally on promising companies and made a few sales.

Next he searched for manufacturers' representatives who would add his granite surface plates to their line. He wrote to Chambers of Commerce in various cities asking for the names of manufacturers representatives, and by correspondence became acquainted with some which were regularly calling on firms that might also buy his product. Mr. Velsey states that Chambers of Commerce are mines of information which can be used to good advantage for many purposes. It has been said that the occupation of manufacturers' representative contains a fairly large proportion of questionable characters who may take advantage of firms they work for. Mr. Velsey states that of the considerable number referred to him by Chambers of Commerce he had met with practically none who were not honest, though some were not proficient in his field. He now has 26 manufacturers' representatives selling his surface plates on a commission basis.

Next he sought a distributor who would take over the entire job of selling, collecting, and corresponding with manufacturers' representatives and customers. Only occasionally, as some special problem arises, does Velsey correspond with his representatives or with purchasers of his product. His present distributor was located through a mutual acquaintance. He is an individual with an office staff of 6 or 8, who personally looks after all his accounts, and is satisfactory. Thus Mr. Velsey is relieved of nearly all selling problems, and can concentrate on production.

He has found that in direct mail advertising, especially to large firms, mail sent only to the firm or to the purchasing agent is almost wholly wasted. It should be sent to the person most directly interested. Often it is difficult to locate those individuals. A manufacturers' representative on visiting a plant can search out just the right person to talk with.

(A successful manufacturers' representative selling machine shop equipment said that on going to a plant he seldom began by talking with the purchasing agent. Rather, he went into the shop and talked with the men who would actually use what he had to sell. When these men thoroughly understood the product and had a desire to use it he would go next to the immediate supervisor of these men and would repeat the process. This would be continued until he had worked up to the purchasing agent. Then, when the purchasing agent inquired in the plant as to the need for making the purchase, he would find no sales resistance, but an eager desire for the goods in question. So successful was this man that his commissions amounted to more than the salary of the president of the company he represented.)

Dewine and Hamma were two small-town young men out of a job. It was a very simple and direct course they took in going from farm to farm in the surrounding country to buy the farmers' eggs and to sell stock feed and farm seeds. Because they gave good, honest service they came to be trusted and counted on. Because they were intelligently on the watch for ways to give better service, their business grew until now it has the largest gross income of any industry in the village. Without advanced education or technical training, they had to build simply on the everyday qualities of common sense judgment, courtesy, honesty, thrift, industry and persistence.

The Antioch Bookplate Company, initiated by college sophomores, had no easy way to begin to make sales. The student in charge travelled from town to town, persuading book stores and gift shops to stock the products. For a few years that and short ads in the book sections of the *New York Times* and *Herald Tribune*, and in the *Saturday Review of Literature*, provided the major means for making sales. In later years some of their special lines, such as religious goods, were sold through jobbers who located their own dealers. At present, in addition to selling through jobbers, some of the territory is covered by members of the Bookplate Company staff, as this keeps the company in touch with the market. Other territory is covered by sales representatives who carry the Bookplate Company line along with others.

Cornelius Grinnell started his career as wholesale distributor for specialized farm power equipment by selling farm elevators. Having persuaded the manufacturer to let him act as retail agent, he took his farm elevator to seven county fairs and to the Ohio State Fair. During the course of three months he sold 75 of the elevators at $500 apiece. This so pleased the manufacturer that he made Grinnell sole wholesale agent for Ohio. With a good record for selling that machine it was not difficult to secure other statewide wholesale agencies, until he is representing thirty manufacturers. At first Grinnell himself visited dealers and persuaded them to carry his lines, but now he needs three full time salesmen to visit dealers over the state.

When Read Viemeister came to Yellow Springs and undertook to develop a practice in industrial design he was fortunate in having a few unfinished jobs in New York which carried him for a time. He made the acquaintance of Richard Odiorne who had started his advertising agency, and did some art work for him. Through Odiorne he met members of a number of manufacturing firms, and picked up a few commissions from them. In his spare time he taught art design at the Dayton Art Institute, and there met a number of industrialists who were actively interested in the Institute. From some of them he received other jobs.

From this point on his work has come from word of mouth contacts. One client tells another. Viemeister has not advertised, nor has he visited industries to introduce himself. After five years of this informal, spontaneous proceedure, as his staff grows there is increased need for an even flow of work and for more of it, and Viemeister plans to spend considerable time in introducing the firm to prospective customers.

Richard Odiorne, wishing to work at advertising, joined a man who shortly before had started an advertising practice in Dayton. This man later decided to move to another part of the country, whereupon Odiorne purchased his interest and moved the business to Yellow Springs. At first he found it necessary to vigorously solicit clients. Among the earlier accounts was a large and important firm, and the manner of handling this account led directly to another important client in a related but not competing field. With these connections to give standing to his company he could more effectively ask other firms for business. Then commissions began to come without his seeking them, and for the past year and a half the firm has done no soliciting of business.

When Robert Metcalf opened his Yellow Springs studio he had one unfinished order from his former practice. Since he had worked in New York, New Jersey and Pennsylvania he was not unknown in his field. A job at Alexandria, Virginia, and one at Middletown, Ohio, came from an acquaintance made through the Dayton Art Institute. A commission for the Mayo Clinic at Rochester, Minnesota, resulted from a lecture he gave at St. Paul. A lecture for the American College Association on Long Island was followed by a commission there. Otherwise his work has come as a result of people seeing his windows, or because people who know of his work have told others. He has not advertised or solicited commissions.

When Major Foote undertook to build a practice in industrial design he was inexperienced in the field, and had to discover for himself how to find clients. He made a few designs to show what he could do. Then he explored Thomas' *Directory of Manufacturers* for firms in and about Ohio that would seem to need art design for their products. He visited these and showed his designs. Before long he was busy. As his work has developed, rather than make designs in general and then try to find someone to buy them, he undertakes to work with a client to find out just what he wants, and then to design with a definite object in view. He finds that clients appreciate businesslike dealings on the part of an artist, so his years in industry have a valuable carryover.

The way Paul Dawson got his start need not be repeated here, except to quote his remark that whatever the circumstances may be there nearly always is a way to handle them.

"SHAKESPEARE UNDER THE STARS." ALL THE HISTORICAL PLAYS WERE GIVEN IN SEQUENCE IN THE SUMMER OF 1952. THE STAGE USES THE FRONT STEPS OF ANTIOCH HALL.

Chapter XIII

BERNE, INDIANA, ANOTHER CASE OF SMALL TOWN INDUSTRIES

Yellow Springs being the site of a college, some persons may assume that without such source of guidance, encouragement and technical skill a small community could not develop a considerable number and variety of little industries. As an illustration to the contrary it may be interesting to refer briefly to the experience of another little town not far away and similar in size, where no such resource existed.

The village of Berne, Indiana, is about as far from a large city as it is possible to be in that state. It was a farm center, settled by Swiss Mennonites. Berne had been losing its young people. There were too many boys and girls on the farms. In town there were already plenty of stores and services to take care of the farmers. Not that the folks were hard up; the land was good and the people honest, hardworking and thrifty. But what young person wants to "stick around " if not needed?

In many towns this drifting away of young people is taken for granted as something that cannot be helped. But the people of Berne were troubled about it. Wasn't there something their young people could make or sell, and live at home? There seemed to be no raw material to manufacture, and almost nobody seemed to have any special skill.

Then someone suggested that the young women knew how to sew. The outcome was that they bought some sewing machines, fixed up a barn to work in (the same old story), and began making men's overalls. Before long they had quite a business. But the overall field was very competitive. Searching for a more profitable line they began making boys' play and school togs. Perhaps extra good quality would give them a market.

They found that mothers seldom looked at the label on a boy's apparel. How could they get boys and their parents to associate good quality with "Winner Brand," the name they had chosen? Here they did some good honest social thinking. What would really benefit the buyer of the clothes and fix the name in his mind?

The answer was, "The Safety Legion." They would teach boys to avoid accidents, which for children are the most frequent cause of death in our automobile and machine age. With every boy's outfit went an invitation to join the "Safety Legion." The boy was sent a membership card, with a magazine of contests on safety. As he sent in answers to the contests he could earn cash prizes and other rewards and promotions. That made learning about safety popular by making it fun. Parents were glad to have their boys get such training. When another garment was needed, the name was remembered as well as the good quality. This little business now employs about 125 people.

Yet still some of the young folks were leaving home. Someone suggested that since they raised cattle and had hides, they might make leather-covered furniture. They fixed up another barn and went to work, getting their patterns from one of the country's foremost furniture designers. Soon they were making some of the highest quality living-room furniture. But still there were surplus young people. So they started another factory for medium-priced furniture, and then a third one for a popular-priced line.

Other little industries followed. Berne ice cream is sold over eastern Indiana. The local printer began to publish books. One firm continues to make men's work clothes. Two hatcheries are active.

So in this little town of 2500 people there are 800 to 1000 on the payrolls. Many drive in from nearby farms. When increase of business called for more employees it was found that there were no more surplus young people. They might have imported labor, but then their town might lose some of its distinctive character of friendly neighborliness. So they started a branch factory in a nearby town where there were surplus workers.

What did Berne have that so many little towns lack? Was it leadership? Community Service, Inc., has made studies of many small communities and their little industries. They find that the leadership needed is no mysterious quality. Just ordinary, intelligent, devoted people getting together and doing their best, with such advice as they can secure, will commonly do the job.

One marked difference can be observed between the industries of Yellow Springs and those of Berne, Indiana. Most

Yellow Springs products go to a limited market, to manufacturers, or to college or university or government laboratories, where there is a high degree of discrimination as to quality, and where the market cannot easily be captured by big advertisers. Even farm seeds, sold by the Yellow Springs firm in carload lots, are used by farmers who know well that price is secondary to quality, and who respect a reputation for excellence. Nearly all products of Berne industries, on the other hand, are used by the none-too-discriminating general public. Big-scale national advertising, high-pressure selling, large banking and credit facilities, chain stores and certain entrenched habits of sharp dealing, put small business at a disadvantage. The Berne industries, more than those of Yellow Springs, find big business menacing to their success. Mr. C.T. Habegger, head of the "Winner Brand" firm making boys' clothes, feels that coercive and monopolistic methods in big business should be met by a strengthening of fair trade laws and by public policies favoring small-business. The difference between Yellow Springs industries, most of which are inherently small-scale, and Berne industries, which are in the field of mass production, may well be kept in mind in the planning of small community industries.

Yet, the success which has been achieved at Berne in fields where mass production is general gives evidence that even such fields are not closed to honest, intelligent thrift and energy.

Another difference may be noted between Berne and Yellow Springs. At Berne nearly everything is "home grown." Nearly all industries were started by natives of the community, and the products are within the reach of general intelligence and competence, without special technical education. At Yellow Springs to a much greater extent industries are built on such education, research and technology, or on strong artistic ability. Not only have the Yellow Springs industries held a considerable part of the home folks, but they have brought into the community a type of people who demand a well-developed cultural environment. The central policy of Antioch College, that education, whether of scientists, engineers, businessmen or professionals, shall be concerned with the development of the entire personality, and shall include both liberal and practical education, seems to have had an effect.

Not that Berne has been unattentive to social and cultural interests. The men's glee club, which has continued for twenty years or more, has developed high quality. The town has evolved its own form of social gathering. Groups of people get together informally for an evening, without program or refreshments and not just for gossip, but for conversation and discussion. It is not only jobs, but the quality of the town, which holds the young people.

Successful industry at its best is but a phase of successful living. When we see what interesting results can follow from such halting and tentative efforts as those in the towns we have described, it would seem that a general awareness in our country of the qualities which make for all-round personal and small-community life would result in a large number of communities which are such interesting and desirable places to live that the survival of the small community, and its cultural and economic prosperity, would be assured.

THE CASCADE IN GLEN HELEN IN WINTER

Chapter XIV

THE SHORTCOMINGS OF SMALL INDUSTRY

A lady asked Mark Twain how she could recover her declining health. He advised her to quit smoking, drinking and swearing. When she said she did none of those things, he commented: "Poor lady, she has no capital to work on." From this point of view small industry has a large backlog of possibilities. True, some of the best management practice in the world is found in American small industry. For excellence of product, successful price competition, high wages, good working conditions, and good profits, some of them are not excelled, and are seldom equalled, by big industries. Yet, by and large, small industry survives in spite of failing to make the most of its opportunities. It fails to take and to hold its optimum share of the total business.

This failure is not due chiefly to inherent incapacity of its owners or managers, but to the fact that there has not existed a creative pattern of social action which they could adopt and follow. Men's creative capacities commonly lie dormant until their social and economic setting provides both a pattern and a stimulus for action. Michael Pupin was an immigrant from a small Balkan country where science was almost nonexistent, and which in modern times probably never had produced a great scientist. Coming to America, his bent for original inquiry was stimulated by the American intellectual climate and was provided with a pattern to work by, and he became a great physicist. Probably some of his countrymen have had somewhat similar possibilities, but never came under the circumstances which stimulated their realization. This illustrates the fact that usually only in an environment which provides a favorable pattern and incentive do men come to see their possibilities and strive to fulfill them.

The American atmosphere has stimulated men to mechanical and scientific achievement, but has not made them *socially* creative to a similar degree. This is true not only of industry, but of American life in general. In local, state and national government how little we have created in 150 years, except the city manager form of government and interstate authorities!

The social philosophy and social organization of most small industry is still rudimentary. Our small industrialists, as well as many larger ones, have been so busy with the day's travel that they have not taken time to question the conventional destinations. The current business environment has not provided a stimulating social pattern. Many men of keen mind and abounding energy have brought into being marvels of small industry, but have not taken time to relate them to their life purposes, or even to see how to overcome some of their characteristic limitations. Because the American society and industry did not incite them to socially implement their achievements, American small business as a whole has fallen far short of its possibilities. Let us consider some of these shortcomings.

The Need for Specialized Services

By far the commonest cause of failure of small industry is "bad management." However, it does not necessarily follow that management is unintelligent or lax. There are many elements which must be handled with fair competence if a business is to succeed, and failure in any one of them may bring threat of disaster. A man may have established an industry out of his inventiveness and skill, but may be weak in selling, or in financial policy, or in labor relations. Only an occasional man is strong in all elements of business administration.

Big industry provides itself with specialized services in many fields. It has its research in engineering and marketing, its financial advisers, its personnel department, its sales organization, and various other services which extensive operations make feasible. Small industry cannot duplicate these in its own staff. Yet in some way it must secure their equivalent or live under a continuous handicap. Especially is this true of modern industry in which the free and easy ways of the past are giving way to more exact knowledge and closer controls. This dilemma leads many an able person to seek employment in big industry where he can use his special abilities, as in selling, or in product development, or in financial control, or in employment relations, rather than to try to exercise all the functions of management in an industry of his own.

Some progress has been made toward meeting this need of small industry for specialized services. Some small industry fields have united for common advertising. A few others maintain common research institutes. Associations of some small industries provide clearinghouses of information for their members. The federal and some state governments provide small industry advisory services, somewhat following the precedent of the county agricultural agents.*

The general industrial and professional structure of our country supplies some of these specialized needs of small industry. This is becoming true in the field of accounting, and many public accounting firms definitely aim to supply such needs. Commercial or nonprofit research laboratories are increasingly used to solve specific problems, but are less commonly available to maintain intimate association with an industry to search out its best possibilities. Other consulting organizations are available to handle problems in advertising, styling, sales methods, packaging, etc. These are most used where an industry already knows that it has a problem, and needs help beyond its usual resources.

In a few lines small industry has had excellent services available for selling. This is notably true as to scientific laboratory equipment. The users of such equipment cannot be familiar with the merits of every small company which makes some special device. They need to rely on the advice of some person or organization which does thoroughly know the field. Several large supply firms, through long years of honest, efficient, and prompt service, with the unfailing practice of making good any defective item, have come to be quite fully trusted by purchasers of laboratory equipment. When a small manufacturer of some special product has demonstrated to one of these distributing firms that his product fills a real need, that it is well made, and that responsible service will be rendered, and when it is accepted for listing

---

*It is commonly assumed in America that the only way to get an effective agricultural advisory service is to have it furnished by government. Danish custom provides a striking contrast. There groups of about a hundred farmers privately organize and employ agricultural advisers. There are hundreds of such groups. These advisers are said to become so thoroughly acquainted that they know the individual records of every cow on every farm they serve. Moreover, they are in such close touch with national and international markets and market controls, and with each other through their own organization, that they are able to advise their clients very quickly of changes which would affect crop planning. As a result, the Danish farmer, without government controls, makes much more sensitive adaptation to changing international conditions than does the American farmer. The latter, while denouncing government interference, runs to the government for controls much more than does the Danish farmer, and apparently with less satisfactory results. Is it not possible that small industry advisory service would also be more satisfactory if maintained by small industry than if supplied by the government? In fact, small industry advisory service also is privately maintained in Denmark.

by such a firm, that product may be generally purchased on the reputation of the distributing firm which carries it. Such methods are used in a number of industrial fields, and could have much greater extension.

Small industry in the aggregate has numerous other sources of specialized counsel. The salesman who comes to a small plant may bring a range of ideas and information gathered on his rounds. The banker gives friendly advice, as does the certified public accountant on his annual trip. Industrial conventions disseminate ideas. The periodical literature of an industry is constantly searching for worth-while suggestions. Commercially published books and government bulletins are available. Yet, even though nearly every kind of specialized service is somewhere within reach of industry, management cannot spend all its time reading or in searching for the organizations which would help. Moreover, specialized consulting services are expensive. To have too many of them around would be confusing and cumbersome. The fact that they are somewhere to be had does not fully meet the needs of small industry. The very variety of services available may be confusing. Creative ingenuity must find a better answer.

In Finland I observed a type of small industry organization which to a remarkable degree seemed to meet the need for over-all specialized industrial service. More than a hundred independent, small metal working firms, each employing from five or six to two or three hundred workers, formed a cooperative central service organization known briefly as "M.T.H." for supplying every kind of industrial service to its members. This center has a permanent staff of about forty, including engineers, research men, accountants, architects, personnel men, and persons to arrange bank credit,

THE MORRIS BEAN & CO. FOUNDRY

government export and import licenses, etc. This central office also knows where to find other specialized services if they should be needed. Each cooperating firm pays a percentage of its gross receipts to maintain the service. Sometimes a job too big for any one of the member firms has been broken down and divided among several.

The manager of a member firm need not waste his time hunting for the specialized consulting services he needs. He simply calls the central office, tells what his trouble is, and relies on it to do anything necessary. In these ways many little firms have the advantage of varied, specialized services and a continuity of interest which otherwise would be quite beyond the reach of any of them. The whole group progresses in technology and in knowledge of business practice.

With the large number of small industries in America, why could not groups of them similarly unite? If small industry will use in effective social organization some of the creative imagination it has long displayed in more conventional phases of business it can greatly improve its competitive position with respect to big industry. Another illustration will reinforce this opinion.

The general public cannot know the respective merits of a vast number of little industries and their products. For its protection it buys well-known brands, which usually are sold by the larger and better known firms in the industry concerned, but which may not be the best. Several years ago, I was informed at the time, the Educational Buyers' Association painted test surfaces with a large number of brands of varnish, and then had the brands rated by a gathering of paint salesmen who, of course, did not know which they were rating. The brand which rated lowest was one most widely advertised and widely used. The salesman for that brand himself rated it lowest, not knowing that it was his own brand. Dominant advertising may, and in some cases does, unduly influence the market. Is it possible for the small, little known industrialist to get a market for his product commensurate with its quality and price?

Should it not be feasible for a large number, perhaps a thousand or more, of small producers to unite and to set up an organization for rigorously honest appraisal, for accurate and representative descriptions of products, and for advertising, using a common brand name? Then it would not be

necessary for each small firm to fight its individual way to
public acceptance. The common brand name would be assurance
that the descriptions and claims of the products were accurate and representative. The public would welcome such a
responsible guide to quality.

These suggestions are but hints of the kinds of solutions
which might be developed to overcome the handicaps of small
as compared with large industry. Adequate solutions will
require both imagination and a spirit of cooperation. The
small industry person has characteristically been a strong
individualist. That is because he was born and reared in
that kind of social climate. Should that climate change,he
might get more satisfaction out of working with others in
similar fields than from his solitariness in industry. In-
terestingly, it is in individualistic France that many
"communities of work" have developed in which group endeavor
has reached a high level. Some men are climate makers.

The day of industrial isolation is passing. While much
small industry may survive and prosper by sheer go-it-alone
independence, to an increasing degree the choice of the
small industrialist will be between interdependence among
equals, or absorption by big business, with the resulting
status of superior and inferior, or operation directly by
government. For a considerable part of American business the
problem is not the superiority of large over small technical
units, but of the social and spiritual climate which pre-
vails. To some extent the slogan, "United we stand, divided
we fall" applies to independent small industry. Small industries can survive better if they will cooperate.

The Problem of Succession in Small Industry

One of the commoner reasons for the decline or extinction
of small industries, or for their absorption into larger
ones, is that as the owner-manager grows old or dies there
is no one left who is equipped to continue its effective administration. Or, the owner or his family may wish to realize
on what they consider to be a family property, and therefore
may sell it to a promoter or to a big industry. Many an
industry, after being sold out of the hands of those who
created it, is bought, sold or traded in the financial world
as though it were a piece of real estate.

This habit, of treating a small industry as though it were a piece of personally owned private property, is injurious to the welfare of the industry involved and of society. Even though one person has been the chief creative factor in building an industry, the development has been a social undertaking in that a number of persons have participated in it. Sometimes the originator and legal owner does not share the policy-making, management and responsibility with anyone else. Since the workers have no part in policy-making or ownership, the industry may not have a strong hold on their loyalty. It is under such conditions that when the owner dies or wishes to retire no one within the organization is ready to take his place.

If the originator or legal owner of an industry sees it for the social undertaking it is, he will seek for employees who have character and competence to share in policy-making and management. He will work for employee ownership and participation to whatever extent the employees are persons of the requisite competence and character. He will train others in management so that he will no longer be indispensable. Then, when the time comes for him to retire, the business can continue, often with no faltering in its quality. The accumulated skill and mastery need not be lost. The workers' homes, and the long-time community relationships, need not be disrupted as is now so often the case with the sale and moving of an industry.

A small industry should be treated as an undertaking in which the originators or legal owners, the investors, workers, the community in which it is located, and the customers, all have equities, none of which will be arbitrarily disregarded. For these relationships to be recognized may require a new social and moral climate. Among the results of such recognition would be that understudies for management would be trained, that the industry would not be drained of necessary resources, and that commonly it would be continued as an independent, going concern, rather than be sold to a promoter or to a big corporation.

We have indicated some of the shortcomings of small industry. There are other difficulties that they alone cannot remove. Among these are tax laws which largely prevent them from financing their own growth. Such tax laws are among the greatest handicaps to the starting of small business. War contract conditions commonly compel small industries to

serve as subcontractors to big ones. Big industries often
are heavily subsidized in building defense plants, and then
are often able to buy vast installations for very small sums,
for use in general manufacture, giving them artificial competitive advantage. Big industry does not hesitate to run to
government when it wants help, as in case of tariff legislation. Small industry should not be criticized for seeking
legislative relief from actual exploitation and from arbitrary hardship imposed by legislation. To correct some of
these handicaps public policy should supplement private efforts.

One of the menaces to small industry is the professional
promoter. If the voting stock of a small industry is widely
distributed, a firm of professional promoters may quietly
buy up a control, and suddenly take over the management of
the industry, which then becomes a pawn of traders and spec-
ulators, its stock being sold to the general public at inflated
prices. Thereafter the promoters have no more regard for the
long time interests of the industry which they have captured
than has a wolf for its prey. This practice of promoters
of capturing and manipulating industries is one of the most
unlovely phenomena of our national business scene.

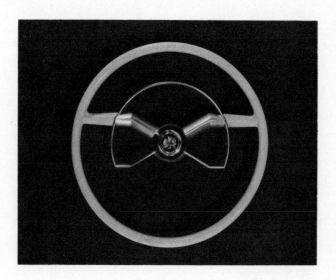

CHEVROLET STEERING WHEEL BY VIE DESIGN

Chapter XV

THE PROBLEM OF SIZE

The problem of size concerns not only business and industry, but every phase of human society. In human relations it has an importance which seldom is fully realized, and calls for a thoroughness of consideration it seldom receives.

Whether in business, government, church or labor union, bigness rarely criticizes itself. How seldom does a man repudiate a regime in which he has a position of exceptional power and advantage! Rather he approves and defends the size and power of his own, and criticizes any regime which threatens it. Big business disapproves and criticizes big government, calling for the return of the good old days of " freedom. " It also criticizes big unions or "labor monopoly. " Big government similarly criticizes big business, and constantly tries to harness it and bring it under control. The big church in its day sought to extend its own range and power, and to curb big government. Bigness in any form tends to surround itself with an aura of virtue, necessity and value. When we consider bigness in business we are dealing, not with an isolated phenomenon, but with one phase of a universal human problem.

The appearance in recent thought and literature of the problem of size and power and their control is witness of the dawning recognition of this issue. The present turbulent emergence of the era of the new technology, the growing determination of oppressed peoples to throw off their yokes, and the prevailing confusion of political, social and economic thinking, indicate that the problem will remain to some extent unfinished business for a considerable period. Nevertheless we do well to search for principles of action which will be valid, at least in the areas of our major concerns.

It is necessary to distinguish between *bigness* of nations, corporations, or other social units and a condition of *interrelatedness*. Before the world wars England and Germany were probably each other's best customers. They were interrelated but not combined in one political or economic organization. The machine tool industry and the automotive industry are much interrelated, but are largely in separate economic organizations. In contrast, the Czarist Russian Empire included a vast territory, but between some of the parts there was far less interrelation than between England and Switzerland, which were separate sovereignties. Human societies are becoming generally more interrelated. That is the desirable and almost inevitable direction of civilization, despite "iron curtains," but interrelation can be a characteristic of either large or small political, social or economic units, or of mixtures of large and small units. Large size does not necessarily mean excellence of interrelation.

One general principle concerning size of human organizations can be well maintained--it is that *size should be no greater than is necessary for the general good.* Research and experience should aim to discover the points at which size begins to sacrifice the general good to cravings for domiance, eminence, power, ambition or wealth. Growth beyond the optimum limits should be discouraged by a sense of ethical responsibility, by public opinion, and by public policy. The prevailing impression that increase of size naturally and generally results in increase of efficiency and of social value should have competent, critical examination.

Bigness in Industry

In the determination of optimum size of industry, profits and prices should not be the only guides for measuring the general welfare. Such matters as undue concentration of population or of power should be considered. For such standards as to size, there would in some cases be no desirability of enforcement by legal means. The same is true with reference to some of the most highly regarded of our ethical standards, such as the "golden rule." Their value often lies in their furnishing guides to voluntary action. In the industrial world only a change in the industrial and social climate would be necessary to bring about a condition in which the determination of industrial policy would generally be based on the total social and economic effect of a course, rather than on the matter of profit alone. To no small degree that is the case today, though if stated bluntly in words, such a standard would be held by some people to be Quixotic. In some respects much business has better standards than it will freely confess to.

There may be elements of American industry in which large size is imperative to excellence of service and to economy. The railroads, the telephone industry, the automotive industry may be examples. To recognize the value of bigness where it is essential is just as necessary as is limitation of size where optimum limits have been reached or exceeded. To break up organizations which inherently call for large size may mean social loss.

However, bigness in American business and industry has become a vogue and a folkway to such an extent that maximum size does not necessarily indicate maximum social value. If the genius of America which has found expression in achieving large size had expressed itself in discovering and attaining economic production on the scale which is socially most useful, the whole structure of our industry might be different, and more rather than less impressive in total results.

In many instances excellence of interrelations of relatively small units may be at least as effective in contributing to the total national economic power as would large size. The machine tool industry is at the very heart of American technological efficiency. Few if any elements of our technology have contributed more effectively to the national defense. If that industry had happened to be concentrated into two or three big organizations we would take that fact to be proof of its necessity, and would not see how American superiority in machine tools could exist without great size. Yet in fact few other American industries are so divided in-

ANTIOCH SCIENCE BUILDING, WHERE SOME SMALL INDUSTRIES WERE HATCHED.

to a large number of independent firms and plants. The industry
is probably more progressive and creative, and contributes
more to the technological dominance of America, than if it
had been highly centralized.

Optimum size for any industry is not something fixed and
static, which can be decided once and for all. It may vary
with technological developments or with social or economic
organization. The economic unit for making artificial ice
used to be an imposing plant from which ice was delivered,
sometimes for a hundred miles around. Now it is an electric
or gas refrigerator in the housewife's kitchen.

Not all of modern trends are toward necessary increase in
size. The standardization of units, parts and types, promoted
by the great engineering societies, the improvement of coor-
dination and interrelation between independent units, and
often the developments of technology, in some cases may remove the former necessity for large size. The universal
availability of electric power in large or small units is in
many cases an influence toward decentralization.

Various social developments are in process which tend to
reduce some of the former disadvantages of bigness. Among
these are the emerging patterns of economic checks and balances. A modern large corporation such as the American Telephone and Telegraph Company or the large railroads or power
companies have many such checks against arbitrary action.
Government supervision is real and in considerable degree
effective. Labor unions demand good wages and working conditions. The very many and widely scattered investors call for
dividends, so that wasteful administration means loss of
investment market status. The customers call for good and
economical service. The general public is inclined to be
suspicious of big business and to listen to criticism. Among
all these pressures management must feel its way, and seldom
can long survive its own arbitrary or irresponsible action.
These checks and balances are far from mature and adequate,
but their steady increase amounts in the total to a wholesome metamorphosis of the capitalist system in America. Yet
even this system of checks and balances has its dangers.
Balances of power have the way of becoming unbalanced.

Economic stresses which on a small scale may be mere public irritants, on a large scale may threaten social stabil-
ity. Giant industry brings forth giant unionism, and these

giants are locked in giant battle. War, whether military
or economic, undermines ethical standards, and the whole
structure of economic society is endangered. The euphemism
"collective bargaining" disguises the fact that we are wit-
nessing a grim contest for the control of our economy. Only
giant government, which is almost certain to act with some
degree of arbitrariness and partisanship, is as yet strong
enough to referee such conflict. The trend is toward courses
of action which infringe upon the democratic process. Here
as elsewhere in human affairs, the control of size is press-
ingly important unfinished business. Time is a factor. The
newly developing checks and balances grow gradually. If consolidation does not take place too rapidly these new controls may save the situation.

We have indicated that well-managed small industry commonly ranks above big industry from the standpoint of profits. However, profits are only one factor to be considered.
No element of our common life can exist as a world by itself.
Such sayings as "business is business," or "art for art's
sake" imply that an activity such as business or art is
properly governed by its own direct interests alone, and
need have no concern for other phases of human well-being.
Such implication is false. Even if it were true that any
particular industry will produce cheaper goods in large
units than in small ones, that alone would not justify large
units. Any given size can be justified only by its total
effect on society.

Looked at in that light there are some heavy counts
against the general prevalence of industrial consolidation
and centralization. It is doubtful whether democracy can

long survive the general consolidation of industry. A man's views of life are mostly the products of his experiences. The average man participates in political life only occassionally. On the other hand, on his job, which is the chief relationship of his life except for his family, he spends eight hours a day, five days a week. In a big corporation the average worker has no part in the making of policies. He does not know, and seldom if ever even sees those who govern the industry. In his job he is part of a non-democratically governed regime. Such a day-in-and-day-out, year-in-and-year-out relationship, rather than the occasional casting of a political ballot, gives form to his social philosophy. If the average workman for a large corporation belongs to a labor union, again he is a part of a mass organization in which his share in directing policy seems negligible. In most large unions less than 10% of the members take any part in union administration except for paying dues and voting on strikes. The habits and spirit of democracy are not developed in great mass organizations.

We are informed by the radio program, "The People Act," financed by the Ford Foundation, that the largest industrial city in America which was built by and for a big industry achieved the distinction of having the second worst criminal record of any city of its size in America. Practically every income earner in the city is an employee of one great corporation, or serves those employees, and most of them belong to one large union. Both the great corporation in this one-industry city, and the great union to which nearly all its non-supervisory employees belonged, seemed so engrossed with big-scale economic considerations that neither the corporation nor the union had time and interest available to make the city a safe, wholesome and desirable place to live. Organized crime and corrupt officials seemed to rule the town until the housewives went into rebellion. Is not such a condition somewhat the result of economic concentration on a large scale? Seldom do we get such an undiluted case of big industry and big unionism, in their effect on the quality of living.

It must be admitted that small industry also commonly is more or less undemocratic in its internal organization, but the process of gradual and indigenous democratization can be more normal and genuine in small than in large units. Moreover, in the aggregate, small-scale industry develops a larger number of individuals who can speak and act according to their judgment. Widespread distribution of independent responsibility and initiative is important in the maintenance of democracy. In some cases where large-scale and small-scale industry are approximately equally profitable from an economical standpoint, the total of social values may favor small units.

As an illustration of the fact that public policy should be guided by consideration of total social values, not simply by current financial profit to those in control, a typical case is provided by our federal policy with reference to banking. In the United States, interstate branch banking is prohibited by federal statute. The result is that the United States has a large number of independent, locally owned banks, which can deal with local business on the basis of first-hand acquaintance and final responsibility. Canada, on the other hand, has only four or five banks, local interests being dealt with through branch banks. These branches cannot act in important matters, but can only recommend action. It is our information that locally owned American banks are far more interested and helpful in handling local financial problems than are the branch banks of Canada. Here we have the operation of interrelatedness in contrast to bigness. The American small bank is not isolated. It has its correspondent bank in a larger city, available for advice and financial cooperation. It can choose freely which bank it will use as correspondent. Thus it has most of the advantage of bigness, while its community commonly has the service of local citizen ownership, which has the interest of the community at heart. In its more intimate understanding of local needs and its quicker and more sensitive responsiveness to them, it is probable that decentralized local banking adds more to the total strength, vigor and health of American economic life than would centralized banking.

Here, again, theory would tend to follow history. If interstate branch banking had been allowed in America, probably by now we would have a few giant banks with many local branches. Almost certainly we would have built our economic philosophy about that condition, and would believe that only by financial consolidation could America have become economically great. The existing degree of widespread consolidation of business and industry may be only a result of our failure to develop standards of optimum size, and may have little if anything to do with the economic power and vigor of America. We may have built our economic philosophy about an historic accident.

If the genius of America had been more generally directed to discovering and achieving the optimum size of industry, rather than the maximum size, it is strongly probable that the structure of industry and the distribution of population would now be very different. If conscious study had habitually been made as to what are the basic needs and desires of men, and of the ways in which these needs and desires could best be met in communities of human dimensions, it probably would have been possible to combine wide distribution of population, and in many more fields general decentralization of industry, with a high order of well-being. Not only it "would have been possible," but it still is possible to the extent that a clear mental picture exists as to what is desirable and possible.

MAZZOLINI WORKING ON A GROUP OF FIGURES FOR THE STATE OF TENNESSEE.

Chapter XVI

SOME CONCLUDING OBSERVATIONS

Kipling's remark applies to the development of little industries:

There are nine and sixty ways of constructing tribal lays
And every single one of them is right.

Yellow Springs industries have no uniform pattern of origin or of development or of policy. Mr. Vernet saw, what every person outside the tropics sees, that freezing water exerts great force. He said to himself, "Why not make such force do something useful?" and a business developed of more than $1,000,000 a year. Mr. Hammond saw, what millions of people have seen, that some substances absorb moisture from the air, as table salt in wet weather, and thought, "Why not make that characteristic serve a useful purpose?" The result is a business with one of the largest incomes of the community. (One wonders how many others of the phenomena described in elementary textbooks of physics and chemistry have not yet been put to work.) Dewine and Hamma saw the inconvenience of farmers coming to town for bulk seed, and with that for a toehold developed a business of $2,500,000 a year.

Money income is mentioned, it being a standard of measurement commonly recognized. The satisfaction of living and working in wholesome and relatively natural conditions and in a desirable small community does not have standard units of measurement.

No single industrial policy is the one right way. One industry encourages its employees to organize a C.I.O. union. In another and larger one the employees prefer informal, friendly relations without union affiliation. One firm will not use sales representatives, but keeps selling in its own hands. Another does not want to bother with sales, and relies largely on sales representatives. One sells most of its product to a dozen customers, sales to each of these averaging perhaps $100,000 a year. Another has 4000 retail dealers, with average sales of less than $50 a year to each. One firm provides many benefits, including pensions, without cost to employees; another has a sharing of both profit and loss, so that the company and its employees are in the same boat. Some firms are in Yellow Springs because their originators were born there, and some because their founders wanted to get away from the big city. Some were started by men well trained in their fields; others by persons who had to learn the business "from scratch." Some succeeded almost from the start; others only after a long struggle. In one respect all or nearly all were alike: they began with meager resources.

Heretofore much of the promotion of small-community industry has been in the interest of old-time craftsmanship. Those of Yellow Springs accept modern technology as having come to stay, and seek to find a way to share in it, while maintaining the human values of the old community. Except for the habit of many employees of operating family gardens which may be worth 10% of annual cash earnings, they put all their eggs in the one basket of the modern age, and would then try to guard that basket from upset. Any general upset probably would be from causes largely beyond their control. Not all successful communities admit dependence on modern technology. Holmes County, Ohio, not very far from the big cities of Cleveland and Akron, is largely settled by Amish people. Having disapproved modern technology, they farm with horses and not tractors, do not have electric light or telephones in their homes, and dress and live with great simplicity. Yet they prosper greatly, and gradually spread by buying up adjoining farms from their more modern neighbors who have gone in for machinery. Almost nowhere else in America have I seen so many small, independent local industries as in and around the little town of Charm, population 500, in the Amish part of Holmes County. And these little industries persist and thrive in their small way. The great depression in the 1930's caused little real inconvenience in this community. Their little industries include cabinetmaking, watch repairing, flour milling, cheese making, harness making, carpet weaving, community auctions (which have spread from this locality to many other parts of America), woolen mill, sausage factory, machine shop, furniture factory, sorghum and cider mills, hatcheries, sawmills, factories for plywood, door and cement block factories, poultry and vegetable canning and freezing, and coal mining. Part of these many little industries are operated by the Amish, part by persons who have rebelled from Amish restrictions and have gone over to the Mennonites, who welcome technology.

On the whole this Holmes County agricultural and industrial area represents a holding to old ways. However, the

young people are restless under the severe restrictions, and
if general economic breakdown is to come it should be soon,
or it will be too late, for Holmes County will have gone
modern. In fact, unless that breakdown comes fairly soon it
will be too late over the whole world. China is straining
for industrialization. In India a certain part--by no means
all--of Gandhi's followers oppose technical industrialization, but the country is not with that attitude. As Asha
Devi, one of Gandhi's most intelligent and devoted followers,
and perhaps the foremost village worker in India, remarked,
"Every Indian village boy wants a bicycle and hopes to become an engineer." In most Indian universities students in
science and engineering greatly outnumber all the others,
sometimes by as much as four or five to one.

Where then will be the last refuge of the pretechnical
era? As I saw Tibetans tramping on foot across the Himalaya
Mountains with one or two hundred pound loads on their backs,
made up of hand-made craft goods, those hardy, intelligent,
cheerful people might seem to qualify as preservers of the
past. Yet, as they walked about the streets of Indian cities
I suspect that even they were developing cravings for power
lathes, jeeps and electric lights. I doubt whether any spot
on earth is a secure refuge from the relentless advance of
the age of science in industry. Yellow Springs has simply
moved quickly and willingly in that direction.

Were we to trace the development of a thousand little industries over America in as many little towns, we should
find a great variety of conditions and incentives playing
their parts. The continuing technical development of our
country makes possible a continually increasing number and
variety. If our small communities are made wholesome and
interesting places to live, and if we have a spirit of pioneering, many such will choose them as locations.

The bewildering variety of programs and policies of little
industries where people are awake to possibilities is an
illustration of one of the values of non-governmental economic operation. These wide-awake small undertakings are
laboratories in social and economic development. Under government ownership and operation would they not be regimented
into a few standard patterns, as is the post office or the
public school? Given a continuation of our economic freedom,
may we not expect the gradual emergence of industrial methods which will combine wholesome, desirable human relations
with economic efficiency.

One very small swallow does not make a summer. A tiny development like that of the little industries in the little village of Yellow Springs is not presented as answering the problem of small community economics. Yet such a development does throw some light on the issue. There is something worth while in American industry and related activities in between big business and peanut stands. These little industries were not thought out clearly and fully beforehand as elements of a community program. Some thinking was done, but often by people working independently of each other.

There are serious problems ahead for our village. Of a score of little economic undertakings, more than half are growing vigorously, and most of the others are better than holding their own. Today they employ more than 500 people. With about 150 employees of Antioch College, at least the same number of self-employed persons in the village, and more than 100 others employed in stores, filling stations, barbershops, eating places, print shops, and in domestic service; by the village government, the Post Office and the railroad; and with perhaps a hundred employed at nearby Wright-Patterson Airfield; a total of more than a third of the population are income earners. Several of the industries may double or triple their employees in a few years, and the village may grow accordingly.

Then what will become of its small-community characteristics? Already the size is about the maximum for a face-to-

Mr. Vernet finds that if he pays good wages his employees save their money and build homes. This is representative of homes of his white and Negro workers.

face community. The very fact that the village is looked
upon as a desirable place to live--probably the most desirable of 30 or more small towns within equal distances from
Dayton or Springfield--results in a movement of commuters to
the village. May not too rapid or too great growth drown out
the community spirit?

Seldom will such a community wholly free itself from the
prevailing feeling that "bigger is better." The personal
profits which may come from laying out real estate subdivisions, building houses, and selling more goods at the stores,
may lead some persons to hold in contempt the idea that
there are desirable limits to the size of a community. Up to
the present these people have not been promoters. They have
only been keeping up with the urgent demand. But while nearly every Chamber of Commerce and nearly every luncheon club
in America is trying to increase the local population, how
can it be expected that a single village will escape that urge?
To many dynamic leaders the prospect of rapid growth is not
a threat but a promise.

For a vigorously growing small community to try to limit
its growth might do more harm than good. If a town of 2500
tends to become a town of 5000, then perhaps the problem is
to try to make a town of 5000 a real community. And when the
5000 becomes 10,000 should not the same effort be continued?
If there should be 100 or 1000 fine small communities about,
equally inviting to persons desiring full, well-proportioned
community life, then the competition for quality would lead
at least some of those to consider carefully whether they
should encourage uncontrolled growth.

America is still a long way from achieving a philosophy
of community, or a clear picture of what qualities make a
good community, or an understanding of how to manage affairs
to bring about the kind we do want. At best we are still
feeling our way. Yet certain fundamentals of good living
conditions are becoming clear. If we keep those well in mind
we may adjust ourselves and our communities to a wide range
of changing conditions, and yet keep and steadily increase
the essential community qualities. One of these essentials
is varied occupational opportunity, such as is provided by
small-scale industry. Another essential is income which will
sustain a good standard of living. The success achieved by
even the faltering efforts at Yellow Springs is a hint of
the possibilities awaiting intelligent and persistent effort.

SEGMENT OF A CIRCULAR STAINED GLASS WINDOW BY METCALF, IN THE TOWN OF PAUL SMITHS IN NORTHERN NEW YORK.